Unknown Oxford

Secret Stories from Oxford University

Malcolm Horton

London | New York

Published by Clink Street Publishing 2020

Copyright © 2020

First edition.

The author asserts the moral right under the Copyright, Designs and Patents Act 1988 to be identified as the author of this work.

All rights reserved. No part of this publication may be reproduced, stored in a retrieval system or transmitted, in any form or by any means without the prior consent of the author, nor be otherwise circulated in any form of binding or cover other than that with which it is published and without a similar condition being imposed on the subsequent purchaser.

ISBN:
978-1-913568-30-6 - paperback
978-1-913568-31-3 - ebook

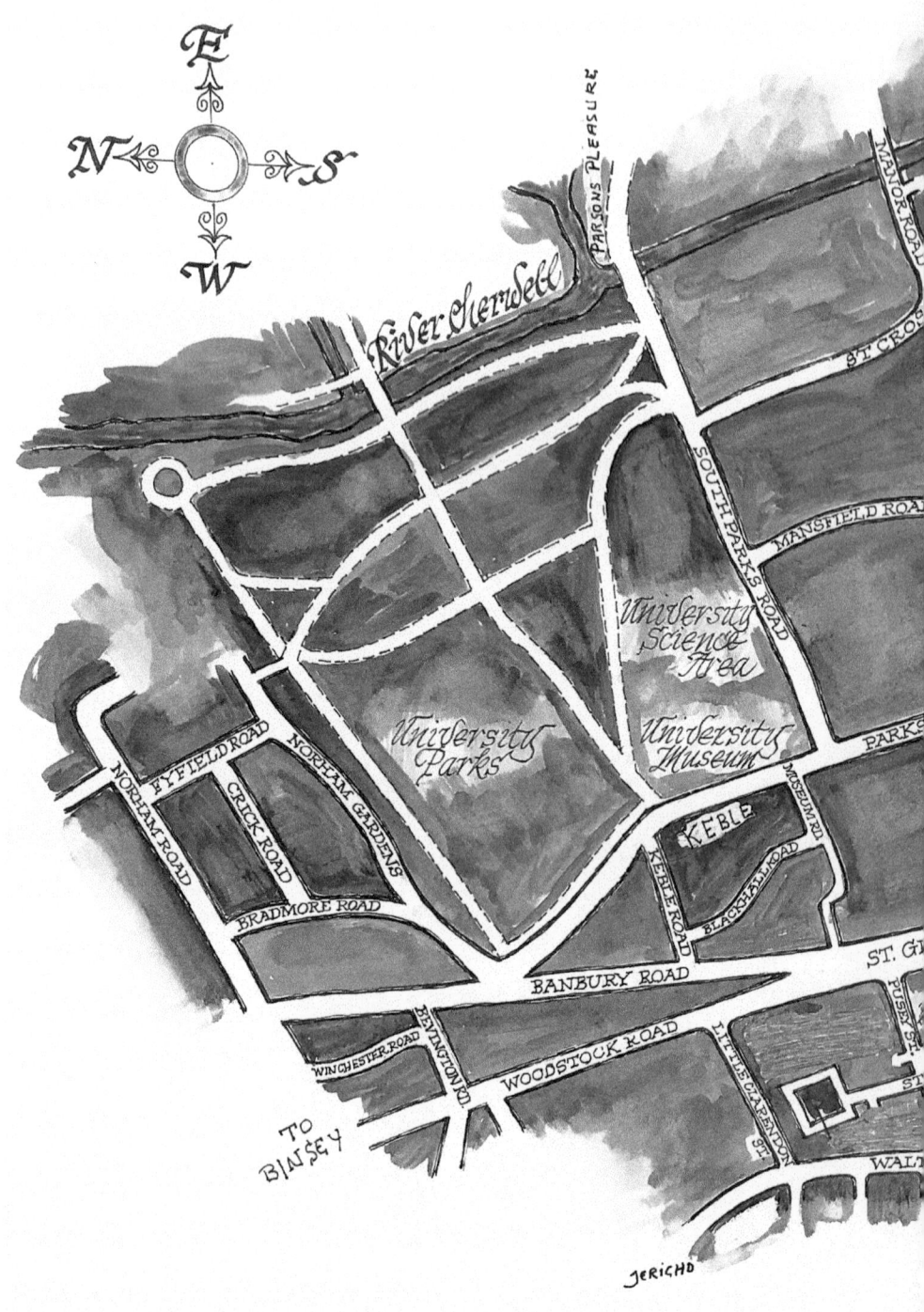

Contents

    Introduction   **11**

1. St Frideswide, Reluctant Bride and Patron Saint   **17**
2. The Other Alfred Legend   **21**
3. The Fair Rosamund – The Love of Henry's Life   **25**
4. Oxford Riots and a Papal Interdiction Spawn the Cambridge University (The Other Place)   **27**
5. The Mallard Ceremony – Once in a Lifetime   **29**
6. The Astronomer Who Came Down To Earth   **31**
7. Elizabeth I – A Hidden Portrait   **35**
8. The Geologist Who Ate a King's Heart   **37**
9. Tragic Cuthbert Ottaway England's First Football Captain   **41**
10. Alice – Wonderland's Femme Fatale   **45**
11. Turner's Cornucopia   **49**
12. 700 Years of Celibacy   **51**
13. The One-Word Essay – The Ultimate Challenge   **53**
14. The Birth of The Oxford English Dictionary   **55**
15. An Outbreak of Crime Writers   **57**
16. Oxford School's Air Heroes   **61**
17. Sir John Masterman University Don and Spymaster   **65**
18. The Bear Inn Tie Collection   **69**
19. Best Council House in Britain   **71**
20. A Degree of Uncertainty   **73**
21. A Tale of Four Churches   **75**
22. Tortoise Racing – The Ultimate Oxford Eccentricity   **77**
23. The Transgender Bursar   **81**
24. Morse and The Case of the Brasenose Knocker   **83**
25. H. M. Postmaster General Bans College Stamps   **87**
26. Dames' Delight and Parson's Pleasure   **89**

27	Zuleika – An Oxford Love Story	91
28	The Hell Raiser from the Valleys	93
29	Light of the World	97
30	Beaumont Palace – Birthplace of Richard Coeur de Lion	101
31	John Deydras – Oxford's Pretender to the Throne	105
32	Summer Is a Coming In	107
33	Religious Turmoil Creates Martyrs and Leaves 400 Dead	109
34	Christchurch Time and Great Tom – Oxford's Largest Bell	111
35	Elias Ashmole – Controversial Founder of Ashmolean Museum	115
36	Cecil Rhodes – Controversial Imperialist	119
37	Gaudy Night – A Convivial Return	123
38	The Black Assizes at Oxford Castle	125
39	Oxford's Unrivalled Coffee Pedigree	127
40	The Dissenting Wesleys – Founders of Methodism	129
41	Deadmans Walk – Ghost Hunters' Delight	133
42	Mary Blandy – Don't Hang Me High	135
43	Woodstock – Sporting Royal Palace	139
44	St Giles' Fair – The Biggest Fair in England	143
45	The First English Civil War	145
46	Oxford – Colin Dexter's Crime Capital of Europe	149
47	Oxford – Royal Capital of England	155
48	Amy Robsart's Mysterious Death and the Virgin Queen's Favourite Courtier	157
49	Britain's Greatest Industrialist and Most Generous Philanthropist	161
50	Treasure from the Caribbean	167
51	British Prime Minister and Chancellor of Oxford University	169
52	A Yank in Oxford	171
53	Blackwells – a Family Institution	173

54 Oxbridge
   A Public Relations Dream   **175**

55 The Downfall of a King and an Oxford Master:
   James II and Obadiah Walker   **177**

56 The Earl of Rochester   The Libertine   **179**

57 The Gay World of Evelyn Waugh   **183**

58 The Killer Queen of Spies   **187**

59 "Women Have a Lesser Brain" Charles Darwin   **189**

60 Adam Von Trott The Rhodes Scholar who tried to Assassinate Hitler   **191**

61 Other Oxfords   **193**

62 A Stroll around the Universities' Colleges   **195**

Introduction

My intention in writing this book is to portray the aspects of Oxford not usually mentioned in the conventional guidebooks. So, I apologise to the reader if I use this introduction to briefly paint a conventional backcloth to the origins and history of Oxford, both town and gown. In that way the reader can be reminded that the 'strange tales' are not set in some fictional fantasy world.

In public perception Oxford is the City of 'Dreaming Spires', celebrated in Matthew Arnold's 1867 poem *Thyrsis*. A city of stunning architecture with its towers, pinnacles, domes and spires dominating the skyline, particularly when viewed from Boars Hill, from the south. All products of the city's university and associated colleges.

Although probably the most famous university in the world, it is not the oldest; that distinction belongs to the University of Karueein in Morocco, founded in 850AD. In Europe the University of Bologna is the oldest, founded in 1088, followed by Paris in 1096.

Oxford for many centuries claimed to be the oldest university with the rather fanciful claim that it was founded by Alfred the Great in 872AD when he was supposed to have founded University College. Although he was a very learned monarch and greatly encouraged learning in others there is no proof that he founded a seat of learning in Oxford.

However, it is now generally accepted that 1167 is the foundation date when Henry II banned English students attending the University of Paris, and Oxford was chosen as their locus academe because of the presence of so many monastic orders in the town with their readymade schools, that attracted the scholars. The Benedictines, Cistercians, Augustinians, Blackfriars, Greyfriars were already established in Oxford, so an academic environment already existed in Oxford.

Situated almost in the middle of England, Oxford is bordered by two fast flowing rivers, the Thames and its major tributary the Cherwell, which rises 40 miles north of Oxford in Northamptonshire. It gained its name from a spot on the Thames shallow enough to allow cattle herders to cross with their beasts; Oxon-ford. It was a place that was exposed, marshy and therefore a somewhat dangerous location. That is why the Romans abjured it as they never settled near fords, preferring to build on higher ground well above the flood plains.

However, the Saxons, with their more maritime background, found Oxon-Ford to their liking, particularly as the Thames was a frontier between two Anglo-Saxon kingdoms, Wessex and Mercia. Their stone-lined river crossing was located near where Folly Bridge now stands on the southern approaches to Oxford.

Oxford first comes into historical legend in the early 8th century when St Frideswide (680-735AD), patron saint of Oxford, founded a priory just north of the Folly Bridge.

However, Oxford first enters recorded history in 893AD when the Anglo-Saxon Chronicles recorded that Alfred the Great constructed one of his defensive burghs at Oxford and, as a result, became a town of great strategic importance.

However, in 1009, tragedy struck in the form of the rampaging Danes in raping and pillage mode. They burnt Oxford to the ground and massacred the monks and nuns of St Frideswide Priory in the process.

As so often in these situations an opportunity was presented to rethink the location of Oxford. It was moved up the hill away from the low-lying Thames crossing point. A fortified town was built with main streets laid out in criss-cross fashion. Each building plot was quickly snapped up by merchants and craftsmen who appreciated the advantages of living under royal protection. Oxford prospered, mainly as a centre for the cloth trade and by the time of the Doomsday survey in 1086 was the sixth largest town in England with 1,016 dwellings. St Frideswide's Priory was rebuilt just inside the south gate, roughly where Christ Church is situated today, and it was not long before many other monastic orders located to the area.

The first 16 colleges of Oxford University, founded between the 13th and 16th centuries, were crammed into the area bounded by the new walls and covered an area of less than 1/6 of a square mile. There are now 39 colleges.

From very early on the local townspeople became somewhat alarmed by these new interlopers from the university who treated them with disdain and thus began the legendary hostility between Town and Gown, resulting in riots and other disturbances. The most serious riots were in 1209 and 1335. Interestingly, the riots of 1209 led to some 3,000 students fleeing from

Oxford to seek sanctuary in Cambridge where they formed a new university (still referred to as 'the other place').

The riots of 1335 were more serious, starting as a commonplace brawl in the Swindlecock Tavern where a group of students complained that the wine was bad. Jugs were thrown and violence broke out, which soon turned into a riot that lasted for two days during which time 63 students perished. King Edward II imposed a fine on the town to be paid in instalments for the next 500 years, on St Scholastica's Day (the anniversary of the day the riot broke out).

By its official charter of 1214 the university had gained many privileges, including the right to administer its own system of justice through the University Chancellor and even had its own police force, the dreaded 'Bulldogs', from 1829 until abolished in 2003. They were supervised by the University Proctors and were one of the oldest police forces in England, recognisable by their distinctive bowler hats.

Things got worse for the townspeople when, in the 15th century, the textile trade moved to the north of England and the university began to acquire land from the impoverished townspeople at knock-down prices. However, the town benefitted by trade and employment from the fast-growing university and eventually tourism.

Today the university employs over 14,000 people and is Oxfordshire's biggest employer. The individual colleges also employ many people in addition. During the English Civil War (1642-46), Charles I chose Oxford as his capital, occupying Christ Church as his campaign headquarters and other colleges for associated activities.

Oxford gained city status when, in 1542, the Diocese of Oxford was created. It was previously part of Lincoln Diocese. The first Bishop of Oxford was Robert King Abbot of Osney Abbey.

In 1908 a young William Morris turned his cycle repair business into a motor manufacturing business with the production of the Morris Oxford. The business was moved out to Cowley, a suburb of the east of Oxford, when it started mass production of cars in 1913; the Morris Oxford being its first mass-produced model. After successive mergers it eventually became British Leyland, employing in the 1970s over 30,000. However, competition from overseas and industrial relation problems saw a rapid reduction in car production and its eventual takeover by BMW who continue to manufacture the iconic Mini, which first appeared in 1959. BMW employs fewer than

4,000 at Cowley.

Town and Gown have learnt to live with one another in relative harmony, recognising that they are inextricably 'intertwangled' in the businesses of tourism and education. This coalescence was recently consolidated when the University Chancellor was granted the Freedom of the City of Oxford and the city's mayor was given an honorary degree.

However, Oxford's beautiful architecture and topography are only part of the fabric of its history. The folklore, legends and fascinating people who have passed through Oxford are of equal importance. The clever, the eccentric, the controversial and charismatic people who have passed through Oxford are part of the history of not only Oxford but the United Kingdom as a whole. It has spawned 27 prime ministers (12 since World War 2) and educated the likes of Oscar Wilde who obtained a double first, John Betjeman who was rusticated (sent down) and left Oxford without a degree. Samuel Johnson famously left Oxford in his second term so did not take the degree examinations. Evelyn Waugh was a student at Hertford and wrote the definitive Oxford novel *Brideshead Revisited*. Children's writers Charles Dodgson, (Lewis Carroll),

C.S. Lewis and J.R. Tolkien were Fellows of Oxford colleges. Two of Queen Victoria's sons, Edward VII and Prince Leopold, were students at Christ Church and Edward, the Duke of Windsor, attended Magdalen.

The list is endless, and the purpose of this book is to tell some of the tales surrounding the extraordinary people who have worked, studied or merely dallied in Oxford that you generally won't find in the many conventional guides published about Oxford.

— 1 —

St Frideswide, Reluctant Bride and Patron Saint

675-730 AD

Frideswide was the enchanting daughter of a Saxon nobleman who lived in Oxford and, not unnaturally, she was considered a great marriage prospect by other Saxon noblemen.

One in particular, the Mercian King, Agar, pursued her with the intention of securing her as his bride. She made it quite clear that he was wasting his time. However, he was not to be thwarted so pursued Frideswide to her Oxford home, where he laid siege. She managed to escape upriver and found refuge in the woods near Binsey, two miles from her home, and for three years lived with a swineherd and his wife leading a simple life working on the land.

According to the ancient chronicles of Robert Cricklade written in the 12th century she soon developed a reputation as a miracle worker; restoring the sight of a blind girl and a fisherman possessed of demons was cured. She gathered around her a group of devoted women. They worked on the land with Frideswide and committed their lives to Christian devotion. To this end they built an oratory and other buildings and dug a well, which Frideswide dedicated to St Margaret. Further miracles took place for those that drank from the well.

Meanwhile, King Agar was not to be deterred even after three years, so he marched his army to the gates of Oxford but was struck blind by lightning in a storm. He somehow came to hear of Frideswide's hideaway at Binsey, so he went to St Margaret's well at Binsey and his blindness was miraculously cured.

According to Cricklade, King Agar immediately realised that his blindness was caused by his overzealous pursuit of unrequited love. He immediately abandoned his lecherous and selfish attitude and allowed the virtuous Frideswide to pursue her life of monastic devotion.

With her unwelcome suitor now out of the way Frideswide returned to Oxford and set up a religious house, St Frideswide's Priory, on the banks of the Thames by what is now Folly Bridge. There it resided after her death until 1009 when the Danish (Viking) raid destroyed it. So it was moved uphill away from the river and inside the South Gate of Oxford's City Wall, roughly where Christ Church Cathedral now stands.

This is where, in the 1980s, archaeologists found a graveyard dating back to the 7th century where St Frideswide is thought to have been buried, and where in 1180 the prior of the monastery with great ceremony made it into a reliquary, which was displayed in a shrine. This proved to be a great marketing move because pilgrims flocked to the shrine, hoping for miracles.

The shrine was broken up during the Reformation in the 1530s. However, many pieces from the shrine have been found during the last 100 years and reconstructed in Christ Church Cathedral. It stands in the Latin Chapel in front of a beautiful stained-glass window designed by the pre-Raphaelite artist Edward Burne Jones in the 1850s. The window depicts various scenes from her life. Her bones had been dug up in the reign of the Catholic Mary Tudor (1553-1558) and kept in a silk bag until a few years later when along came the Protestants. By this time the religious clock had swung back to the Protestants, who accidentally mixed them up with the bones of a recently deceased townswoman and they were reinterred together in the upper part of the church to the east. This is where the shrine is now. The Lady Chapel contains a paving stone in the floor carved simply with the name Frideswide and it is here that the anniversary of her death is commemorated on 19th October each year. Unwittingly, in a Monty Pythonesque scenario the unknown woman whose bones were mixed up with St Frideswide at the time of the reformation is also indirectly venerated. One only hopes she was of good character!

St Frideswide became the patron saint of Oxford in 1440 but she is also commemorated in the graveyard of St Margaret's Church, Binsey, where pilgrims visit her well in the hope of cures and miracles.

The Binsey Well also comes into fiction in amusing fashion in *Alice in Wonderland* as the treacle well. In its mediaeval form treacle was a healing liquid. In the section of the story relating to the Mad Hatter's Tea Party, the tale is related by the Dormouse about three little sisters who lived in a treacle well. St Frideswide's well in Binsey would be well known to Alice in

Wonderland's creator Lewis Carroll (Charles Dodgson), and Alice Liddell and her two sisters from their Sunday storytelling picnics, as Binsey was on the banks of the Thames and the well only a short walk away.

So, one way and another St Frideswide's legend looms large in Oxford's past.

— 2 —

The Other Alfred Legend

872AD

For nearly 400 years University College claimed to have been founded by King Alfred in 872AD and was thus the oldest 'academic minor' of Oxford University. If this were the case Oxford would be the second oldest university in the world after the University of Al-Karaouine in Morocco, founded in 859AD.

This is the second and least known Alfred legend (after the burnt cakes). There is much circumstantial evidence to support this claim, not least that Alfred was largely responsible for the restoration of learning in England after the decay in scholarship precipitated by the ravages wrought by the Vikings. Prior to this, in the 8th century at the time of Bede, England was a great seat of learning.

Alfred was the youngest of the four sons of the King of Wessex. He greatly resented his lack of education, due mainly to the Danish Viking upheaval, so in later life he taught himself Latin and in the last seven years of his life translated five major works from Latin into English, including Pope Gregory's *Pastoral Care*, Bede's *Ecclesiastical History of the English People* and St Augustine's *Soliloquies*.

He was one of the most learned kings to have ruled England and was keen that his subjects should also be educated so that England should be intellectually equal to Europe.

Before he could commence his intellectual crusade, he had to deal with the invasion of the barbaric Danish Vikings who landed with their Great Army in East Anglia in 866. They then set about the destruction of every kingdom in the island from Wessex to Northumbria. In seven years, the Danes had ransacked and destroyed all vestiges of civilised administration and learning.

It is at this point that Alfred the Great, Warrior King emerges. After initial setbacks and a tactical retreat to the Isle of Athelney, in Somerset, he conducted a guerrilla campaign whilst marshalling his Anglo-Saxon forces from not only Wessex of which he was now king but also Mercia, his wife's native kingdom.

Alfred won several decisive battles and forced the Danes back to Danelaw (East Anglia). Importantly he occupied the City of London in 886 so he now controlled Wessex and Mercia. His daughter Aethelflaed married the King of Mercia, thus consolidating the two kingdoms.

Alfred then established key defensive fortifications or burghs of which Oxford was strategically one of the most important, being on the borders of Wessex and Mercia.

He also founded the first English Royal Navy so he could fight the Vikings on their own terms. There then followed his landmark confrontation with Danish King Guthrum whom he defeated at the Battle of Edington in 878 and whom he converted to Christianity. He recognised that to secure a permanent peace he would have to give Guthrum something in return. This he did by granting the Danes equal citizenship and allowed them to keep East Anglia where they settled peaceably.

This created the stability he required to first of all codify the common laws of England which were accepted in Kent and Northumbria as well as Wessex and Mercia. He then set about beginning the process of spreading knowledge amongst his subjects by introducing schools attached to various religious houses.

Alfred delighted in the society of learned men, such as Asser from the Monastery of St David's in Wales and Plegmund, Archbishop of Canterbury.

He helped plan the *Anglo-Saxon Chronicles*, but his Oxford connection was given great substance by two other learned men of this period, one of whom was St Neot a kinsman who, according to Ranulf Higden's *Polychronicon* of 1354, helped Alfred establish public schools in Oxford. The second learned man was Grimbald who represented Alfred's greatest coup in the intellectual transfer market.

Grimbald was as scholarly monk in Flanders where he was in the service of the Archbishop of Rheims. In return for twenty fine hunting dogs Alfred obtained the services of Grimbald who, according to William Camden in 1603, founded in Oxford the Church of St Peters in the East (now part of St Edmund Hall) where he is reportedly buried.

University College has relied on the Alfred connection in two successful lawsuits. One in 1380 invoked the protection of Richard II on the grounds that his ancestor, King Alfred, had founded the college. The second dispute in 1727 in the Court of King's Bench reaffirmed the fact of its Royal Foundation by King Alfred.

In 1872, University College unashamedly celebrated its millennium, crowned by the presentation of burnt cakes by the Regus Professor of History. Since this date the college has been more circumspect in its allegiance to King Alfred, but he is still prayed for on college feast days.

It is inconceivable that Oxford was not his principal seat of learning and we know that by the time Grimbald arrived in Oxford many religious houses were already in existence there. Also he was frequently in the Oxford area, hunting at Woodstock.

Lastly it seems fitting that the famous Alfred Jewel discovered in the 17th century on the Isle of Athelney is now housed in Oxford's Ashmolean Museum. It is the remaining survivor of several ornate bejewelled pen heads that were symbolically presented to bishops in their key seats of learning.

Therefore, University College's fanciful claim does seem to have some substance if no more than a symbolic recognition of his achievement in re-establishing organised learning in England.

— 3 —

The Fair Rosamund – The Love of Henry's Life

1176

Not many mistresses have a shrine built for them by their royal lovers, especially when the lover in question, Henry II, had a wife who was still alive: Queen Eleanor (of Aquitaine).

The Fair Rosamund, renowned for her great beauty, was the daughter of Walter Clifford, a Marcher Lord from Herefordshire and therefore an extra powerful baron.

She met the future Henry II in 1175 when she was 15 and he, aged 32, was attending the opening of Flaxley Abbey in the Forest of Dean.

They were smitten and would have married but dynastic ambition had required the young prince to marry 13 years earlier the formidable Eleanor of Aquitaine, who was 10 years older than he. Henry continued seeing Rosamund and their illegitimate children included William, Earl of Shrewsbury and Geffrey, Archbishop of York.

Rosamund died in 1176 under mysterious circumstances aged only 26 and was buried at Godstow Abbey where she had received her education at the hands of the nuns, and where Henry erected her shrine.

Their affair had lasted for ten years and Henry had Woodstock Palace erected for her in order that they might conduct their affair in relative seclusion. After all, he had a royal palace nearby in Oxford just 10 miles away, Beaumont Palace, built by his grandfather, Henry I, in 1129. In fact, Queen Eleanor gave birth to the future King John at Beaumont Palace in 1166 rather than the newly completed Woodstock Palace. In any case Henry and Rosamund were living in Woodstock more or less as man and wife. She even accompanied Henry on his frequent trips to France.

It was obvious that the tempestuous Queen Eleanor was not going to put up with being cuckqueaned forever. Her revenge is the stuff of legend.

Henry and Rosamund's love nest was not easy to find. It was in a maze on the Woodstock estate. Queen Eleanor was able to locate it by attaching the end of a ball of wool to Henry's coat and following its trail. She waited until Henry had left Rosamund alone before confronting her.

Rosamund was given two options to assist her suicide, a dagger or poison. She chose the latter.

When Henry discovered her body, he was devastated. He was still getting over the death of his one-time close friend Thomas Becket just six years earlier in 1170.

Not only was Rosamund commemorated by the shrine at Godstow, there is also a well named after her on the Blenheim Palace estate which was built to replace Woodstock Palace. Rosamund's well is located south of the Grand Bridge on the western shore of Capability Brown's magnificent lake.

Countless poems were written about the Fair Rosamund and she features in novels written about this period. She is one of the great romantic figures of the 12th century.

In 1189, two years after Henry II had died, the Bishop of Lincoln, safe from the wrath of Henry, had Rosamund's remains removed from the church to the graveyard outside. He did not want a King's mistress honoured with a shrine. However, as soon as Rosamund's son, the Archbishop of York, heard of the Bishop of Lincoln's action he countermanded the order and had his mother 'the Fair Rosamund' restored to her proper place.

Interestingly, the ruins of Godstow Abbey are only a few miles from Binsey, where Oxford's patron saint St Frideswide's healing well is located.

Sadly, the remains of Rosamund's shrine at Godstow were destroyed by Cromwell's Puritans. However, the remains of Godstow Abbey are still extant but Rosamund's lasting legacy is her enduring legend as the love of Henry II's life.

— 4 —

Oxford Riots and a Papal Interdiction Spawn the Cambridge University (The Other Place)

1209

There had been schools in Oxford for most of the 12th century attached to the various monastic foundations: Augustinians, Benedictines, Cistercians, Carmelites and, later, Blackfriars and Greyfriars.

In 1131, Henry I (the second monarchical son of the Conqueror) built Beaumont Palace just outside the north gate of Oxford, roughly where today Beaumont Street and Watton Street meet. King Richard (The Lionheart) I and bad King John, Henry I's grandsons were born in Beaumont Palace.

So, when Henry II, son and father of the above-mentioned, in 1167 banned English students attending the University of Paris, it was reasonable to found England's first university in Oxford. The infrastructure was already in place and royal protection was close at hand. So, Henry II was the de-facto founder of England's first university in 1167.

Unfortunately, this academic idyll lasted only a few short years before Oxford was thrown into total confusion by two unconnected events. Bad King John and Pope Innocent III fell out because the Pope appointed Simon Langton Archbishop of Canterbury. This led in 1208 to the Pope excommunicating King John and laying an interdict on England and, as a result, closing all its churches and schools, including Oxford's Monastic Schools.

And then, in 1209, the first of the so-called Town and Gown riots broke out in Oxford when a young woman was murdered by a scholar who was duly found guilty. He managed to escape, and the townspeople summarily took their revenge by executing two of the culprit's fellow students. All hell broke loose and King John, being somewhat preoccupied with his dispute with the Pope did not intervene.

As a result, about 3,000 masters and students upped sticks and moved to the calmer waters of Cambridge. The unlikely choice of Cambridge came about because the leader of the exodus from Oxford was its Master of Schools, Dr John Grim who was a native of Cambridge. Also, the Bishop of Ely was keen to see a university set up in his diocese. He even founded Cambridge's first college, Peterhouse, in 1284.

A few years later King John, on the advice of the Archbishop of Canterbury Simon Langton, who clearly was now accepted by King John, settled his differences with the Pope and things ecclesiastical returned to normal and further defections from Oxford were halted for the time being at least. Riots between Town and Gown were to be a continual feature of the first two or three centuries of Oxford University's existence, but that is another story.

However, the enduring legacy of Oxford's 1209 troubles was the spawning of England's Second University, 'the other place', Cambridge.

— 5 —

The Mallard Ceremony – Once in a Lifetime

1601

Every 100 years there takes place at All Souls College the somewhat Monty Pythonesque ritual of 'Hunting the Mallard' in commemoration of the chase after a huge duck which flew from the drains during the building of All Souls in the 15th century. Archbishop Chichele who established All Souls is said to have had a premonition about the duck in a dream, hence the chase at the time and the centennial ceremony.

The ceremony involves the college totem, a wooden duck, held aloft on a wooden pole being drunkenly paraded around the college by the fellows every hundred years on St Hilary's Day (14th January). They sing the Mallard Song in honour of the 15th century duck.

Fortunately, the Mallard Song is not confined to the centennial ceremony; it is also sung twice annually, at the Bursar's Dinner in March and the college's Gaudy in November.

The first recorded reference to the ceremony dates from 1632, so one must assume the ceremony was held in 1601.

The next ceremony is not due until 2101 and one assumes the 100-year gap is due to the fact that the college was founded in 1438 to commemorate the dead in the Hundred Year War with France.

The first verse of the Mallard Song is as follows:

> "The Griffin, Bustard, Turkey and Capon
> Let other hungry mortals gape on
> And on their bones with stomachs fall hard
> But let All Souls men have ye Mallard."

— 6 —

The Astronomer Who Came Down To Earth

1663

In the opinion of the 20th century architectural historian Sir John Summerson, if Christopher Wren had died at the age of 30, he would still have been a figure of national importance, not as an architect but as a scientist and astronomer.

By the age of 45 he was Britain's foremost architect. As so often in life, destiny, in the form of a set of curious chances (to quote Gilbert and Sullivan) were the determining factors:

The Restoration of the Monarchy in 1660 and the Great Fire of London in 1666.

Christopher Wren was born in 1632 at which time his father was Dean of Windsor and his Uncle Matthew successively Bishop of Hereford, Norwich and Ely. Both were high church and devoted Royalists. Cromwell imprisoned Uncle Matthew in the Tower of London for 18 years. However, after Cromwell's departure Uncle Matthew was released and returned to his alma mater Pembroke College, Cambridge as Master and, in grateful thanks, built a new chapel appointing, in 1662, his nephew, Christopher Wren, who was something of a polymath, as architect. His first such appointment and thus began his illustrious career as architect.

Later, the Great Fire of London in 1666 and the consequent rebuilding of St Paul's Cathedral and 52 London churches established Christopher Wren's pre-eminence as an architect.

After attending Westminster School, Christopher passed onto Wadham College, Oxford where he graduated before moving onto All Souls as a Mathematics and Physics don. His fertile mind soon expanded into astronomy, horology (the science of measuring time) and anatomy. In 1659 he designed a magnificent sundial, which now adorns the wall of the Codrington Library at All Souls and this was, strictly, his first architectural project. Also, he carried out a series of splenectomy operations on dogs (removing the spleens). He also helped perfect the barometer.

In 1657 he secured the post of Professor of Astronomy at Gresham College in London where he helped found the Royal Society. He and a few of his colleagues at Gresham soon developed an interest in the new profession of architecture with its emphasis on mathematics. Until this time the design of buildings was carried out by the Master Stonemason or Master Carpenter. The word architect did not appear in the Oxford Dictionary until 1583. The

Royal Institute of British Architects (RIBA) was not established until 18

Wren's second significant architectural project was the Sheldonian Theatre in Oxford in 1663/4. Later, Oxford projects included Tom Tower at Christ Church and Trinity College Chapel. In Cambridge he designed Trinity's Library and in London was commissioned by the Dean's Chapter of St Paul's in 1663 to produce a programme of repairs and improvements to the old St Paul's Cathedral. His proposal to add a dome was to cause great controversy. In the event, the Fire of London in 1666 destroyed St Paul's and 52 City churches and provided Wren with his most famous architectural undertaking, dome and all.

Other works soon followed including the Chelsea Hospital, the Royal Exchange, Greenwich Observatory and Greenwich Hospital. One of his final designs in 1711 was Marlborough House, now the Headquarters of the Commonwealth of Nations.

Earlier, in 1669, Charles II appointed him to the post of Surveyor General responsible for all royal and government buildings and their maintenance; a post he occupied for 60 years. He was a particular favourite of Charles II who took a great interest in the work of the Royal Society.

He was knighted in 1672 and became President of the Royal Society in 1684. He even dabbled in politics for a while, being elected Member of Parliament for Windsor in 1689 and Melcombe Regis in 1701.

On a personal level he was twice married and produced four children but neither of his marriages lasted more than four years, his two wives dying of smallpox and TB respectively.

He notionally had a fifth 'adopted child' in Nicholas Hawksmoor, who was a member of the Wren household throughout the 1680s. He was Wren's personal assistant and most talented pupil. He famously designed All Souls Great Quadrangle with its magnificent Codrington Library and its beautiful twin towers, a major feature of Oxfords 'dreaming spires'.

Fittingly, when he died in 1723, Christopher Wren was buried in St Paul's Cathedral.

To quote the title of his most recent biography by Adrian Tinniswood, "His invention so Fertile".

— 7 —

Elizabeth I – A Hidden Portrait

1672

Jesus College in Turl Street has been associated with Wales since its foundation by Queen Elizabeth I in 1571 at the petition of Hugh Price, Treasurer of St David's Cathedral. He provided its first endowments while the Queen provided the site. It is the only Oxford College to date from the Elizabethan period.

In the Hall there hangs, in pride of place above High Table, a remarkable full-length portrait of Queen Elizabeth I by Nicholas Hilliard (1537-1619) – and thereby hangs a remarkable tale.

The painting, given to the college in 1672 by Dr James Jeffreys, an alumnus of Jesus and brother of the notorious 'hanging' Judge Jeffreys, mouldered away for centuries in a dark corner of the Fellows' Library, completely unnoticed and unremarked. It had mainly, in the 18th century, been over-painted and was thought to be a later copy of some unknown contemporary painting and of little value. It was in effect a palimpsest.

Then, in 1994, the art expert, Alec Cobb, was commissioned to clean the college portraits, including the Charles I portrait by Van Dyck. The Fellows' Library painting was not on his list, but Mr Cobb noticed it and was curious. He thought the picture looked interesting and was given permission to bear it away for closer inspection.

After cleaning a section of the painting and submitting it to experts at Christie's and Sotheby's it was agreed that it was certainly the work of Nicholas Hilliard, best known for his execution of portrait miniatures. The provenance of the painting was further confirmed by Sir Roy Strong, an acknowledged expert on the paintings of Hilliard.

Unknown Oxford

The over-painting was painstakingly removed and there in all its glory was a full-length painting of Elizabeth I, and what had been a forlorn picture in a corner was elevated to the status of a national treasure.

Malcolm Horton

— 8 —

The Geologist Who Ate a King's Heart

1848

Canon William Buckland (1784-1856) was a pioneering 19th century geologist and mineralogist who, rather ostentatiously, claimed to have eaten his way through the entire animal and insect kingdom – the anthropoids. He opined that the nastiest thing he had ever eaten was a mole, closely followed by a bluebottle.

An invitation to dinner or breakfast at his house in Oxford would often include on the menu mice cooked in batter, crocodile or, a particular favourite, leopard chop.

However, the most amazing story about Buckland concerned a visit in 1848 to Nuneham Courtenay a few miles south of Oxford, the home of the Archbishop of York, Edward Harcourt. Because of his boast that he could name any meat he consumed by taste alone he was given a shrunken object from a silver cask to sample. To the horror of his host and assembled guests he swallowed the lot. When told that it was the mummified heart of King Louis the XIV (The Sun King) who had ruled France from 1643-1715, he exclaimed, "I have never eaten the heart of a king before!"

As eccentrics go he was definitely at the extreme end; as is so often the case geniuses tend to be somewhat eccentric. He occupied the Chairs of Geology and Mineralogy at Oxford University in recognition of his ground-breaking work in palaeontology. He described and named the first dinosaur from anywhere in the world, remains of which were discovered in Oxfordshire in the 16th century; the Megalosaurus, reckoned to be 167 million years old.

Buckland's early excavations took place in Kirkdale in Yorkshire and Shotover Hill, three miles east of Oxford where he uncovered fossils which found their way to the University Museum.

Another discovery in 1823 was the so-called Red Lady of Paviland, on Goats Hill Cave near Rhossili on the Gower Peninsula in South Wales. At first it was thought to be the dyed skeleton of a Roman female. More recent analysis indicates the bones of a young male dating back to the Old Stone Age period roughly 25,000 years ago.

Buckland married Mary Morland, an accomplished illustrator and collector of fossils in 1825, and on a year-long honeymoon touring Europe controversy and showmanship accompanied them wherever they went. On a visit to Sicily he shattered local folklore by pronouncing that the relics of St Rosalina, in her shrine cave high on the slopes of Monte Pellegrino, were the bones of a goat! The sanctuary was immediately closed. On a visit to Naples to attend the annual liquefaction of the blood of St Gennaro, he kneeled down, licked the blood and declared it was bat's urine.

Buckland studied and was ordained at Corpus Christi College, Oxford and was appointed a Canon of Christ Church, Oxford and in 1845 Headmaster of Westminster. He instituted many reforms and improvements at the school, including the sanitation.

Needless to say, as a lecturer he was a charismatic and controversial figure. His lectures were packed out as he tried to reconcile conventional biblical doctrines of creation with his scientific knowledge.

Around 1850 he contracted a disorder of the neck and brain which progressively disabled him, causing his death in 1856. His eldest son, Frank Buckland, the well-known naturalist, attributed his illness to an accident he had on one of his expeditions.

A memorial bust of William Buckland by the sculptor Henry Weekes, is in the nave of Westminster Abbey with an inscription written by Lord John Thynne which contains the epithet "ensued with the superior intellect he applied the powers of his mind to the honour and glory of God, the advancement of science and the welfare of mankind". He is buried at Islip near Oxford alongside his wife. He donated his entire collection of fossils and rocks to the Oxford University Natural History Museum, founded in 1850, which fittingly, holding centre stage is a replica of the Megalosaurus.

— 9 —

Tragic Cuthbert Ottaway
England's First Football Captain

1850-1878

The world's first international football (soccer) match took place on 30th November 1872 between England and Scotland Cricket Club, Glasgow, witnessed by a crowd of 4,000. The result was a 0-0 draw.

England's captain was Cuthbert Ottaway, a 22-year-old undergraduate at Brasenose College, Oxford. Ottaway had just returned from a cricket tour of Canada and America with the MCC where he opened the batting with the legendary W.G. Grace.

In fact, he was something of a sporting all-rounder having the previous summer represented Oxford University at cricket, racquets, real tennis and athletics and, of, course football the previous winter. In total he made thirteen appearances against Cambridge University at these five sports that is still a record for blues-ranked events, which even the legendary C.B. Fry did not exceed.

In 1874, he captained Oxford University in their FA Cup Final triumph over the Royal Engineers. The inaugural FA Cup competition was in 1872 in which Cuthbert played for Crystal Palace, reaching the semi-finals, losing to the eventual winners the Royal Engineers but, he was to appear in one more FA Cup final in 1875 when he captained the Old Etonians against, once again, the Royal Engineers to whom they lost 2-0 in a replay.

Born in Dover in 1850 to a thoroughly middle-class family (his father was a surgeon) he gained a King's Scholarship to Eton. He was in his element at a time when sporting success at public schools was regarded as 'the measure of the man'. It was not long before he was representing Eton at racquets – an early form of squash and fives – similar to racquets but played with a gloved hand. He also played the Eton field game, one of the many versions of football played at this time. In 1868 and 1869 he won the public school's Racquets Championship.

THE PRINCIPAL AND FELLOWS OF BRASENOSE COLLEGE

However, it was cricket at which Cuthbert excelled and he went on to captain Eton against Harrow at Lords. This was one of the highlights of the sporting and social calendar and, founded in 1822, is the oldest surviving fixture in cricket. In 1867 he was invited to Lords for special coaching. His final term at Eton was to be his golden summer. He scored nine centuries including 108 against Harrow at Lords. This culminated in his selection to play for his native county Kent against the mighty MCC captained by W.G. Grace. He was Kent's top scorer with 55.

Academically Ottaway was no slouch either. In 1868 he won two scholarships from Eton to Brasenose College, Oxford where he studied Classics. As already mentioned, his sporting achievements were many and varied, but it was in association football – soccer for short – that he was to achieve immortality.

Oxford adopted the Cambridge Rules of 1865 that codified the various versions of football and led to the separation of the handling form of the game rugby, made famous by William Webb Ellis from the school of the same name. Incidentally, he was also a student of Brasenose albeit 50 years earlier. Oxford University Football Club was founded in November 1871 six months before the first FA Cup final won by the Wanderers. They appeared in four FA Cup Finals in the next decade, winning in 1874 when Ottaway was captain.

In 1874, having secured a first in Classics he left Oxford to pursue his career as a trainee barrister. He was now based in London and it was natural that he should accept an invitation to play cricket for Middlesex in the summer, whilst in the winter captained the Old Etonians at football who, in their first attempt, reached the FA Cup Final in 1875.

In 1876, Cuthbert qualified as a barrister and in that same year married Marion Stinson from Hamilton, Ontario, whom he first met on the MCC tour to Canada in 1872.

The newlyweds settled down in London where Cuthbert was a practising barrister. Christmas 1877 was spent with his parents in Dover when the happy couple announced that Marion was expecting their first child.

Their joy was short-lived when tragedy struck; late in March 1878 Cuthbert caught a chill after a night dancing and died from chest complications, possibly tubercular in origin. He was only 27 when he died and was buried at Paddington Old Cemetery on 2nd April.

Cuthbert Ottaway was struck down before he even reached the prime of his life. England and Oxford lost one of its greatest sporting icons and the first captain of England's football team, one of the founding spirits of the 'beautiful game'.

As a footnote, Cuthbert's wife Marion gave birth to a daughter Lillian on 22nd July 1878. After a few years they returned to Canada where Marion remarried in 1884.

— 10 —

Alice – Wonderland's Femme Fatale

1852-1934

Alice Liddell, the inspiration for Alice in Wonderland, spent her formative years surrounded by young impressionable males, firstly at Westminster School where she was born in 1852 and then Christ Church, Oxford's premier college.

Her presence at these two prestigious seats of learning was due to the fact that her father, Henry Liddell, was successively Headmaster of Westminster School 1852-1855 and then Dean of Christ Church (Head of House) from 1855 until 1891.

Alice was the fourth of the ten children of Henry Liddell and his formidable wife Lorina.

At this time Oxford University and its twenty constituent colleges was a totally male preserve, populated by 15,000 male students. It was to be another twenty-three years before the first female student was to appear in Oxford. So Alice and her four sisters were literally spoilt for choice.

Alice was naturally at ease in the company of men through the many she encountered at the various college social events she attended as the Dean's daughter. She was a physically attractive girl with an engaging personality.

The first male to fall under her spell was a young maths tutor at Christ Church, Charles Dodgson (Lewis Carroll), whose hobby was photography which at that time was in its infancy and quite an innovation. He quickly endeared himself to the Liddell family by offering to take photographs of the children, his favourite subject being the seven-year-old Alice, with whom he developed a close friendship. He was an intensely shy man who loved the company of young female children.

The photography sessions soon led to Dodgson being allowed to take Alice and her sisters, Lorina and Edith, on boat trips up the Thames to Godstow under the watchful eye of the children's governess Miss Prickett.

Tom Quad, Christ Church, Oxford

After a while the boat trips were enlivened by Alice's insistent plea to "Let's Pretend" and thus began the Alice Stories.

Charles Dodgson exchanged frequent letters with Alice which could be interpreted as love letters and it has even been suggested that a proposal of marriage was contained in at least one of them. When Alice was ten years old, Mrs Liddell somehow got to see the letters and all social intercourse between the Liddell family and Dodgson ceased.

In 1872, when Alice Liddell was 20, Queen Victoria's youngest son Leopold matriculated at Christ Church, following in the footsteps of his elder brother, the Prince of Wales (the future Edward VII) who came up to Christ Church in 1859.

Leopold was a frequent visitor to the Deanery and it was not long before he fell in love with the Dean's enchanting daughter Alice. Mrs Liddell was delighted at the prospect of what she considered a suitable match for the Dean of Christ Church's daughter. However, Queen Victoria thought quite the reverse; a mere commoner was a most unsuitable prospect for a Prince of the Realm.

Leopold was married off to a German Princess but sadly died at the age of thirty. He was a haemophiliac.

In 1878 another Christ Church undergraduate fell for the bewitching Alice; Reginald Hargreaves, a wealthy country gentleman whose favoured pursuits were hunting and cricket. He played for Hampshire and the MCC although his achievements with bat and ball were not impressive.

Alice and Reggie married in 1880 and produced three sons, one of whom she named Leopold and to whom Prince Leopold was godfather. Prince Leopold also named his daughter Alice. Sadly, Leopold Hargreaves and his brother Alan were killed in the First World War. Their third son Caryl (named after Lewis Carroll) served in both the First and Second World Wars in the Scots Guards. He died in 1968.

Alice settled down to the life of the wife of a wealthy country gentleman in Lyndhurst in the New Forest and became a noted society hostess and took to calling herself Lady Hargreaves, although there was no basis for such a title. However, it was a far cry from her glamorous life at Christ Church.

After her husband's death in 1926 she sold her manuscript copy of *Alice's Adventures Underground* (Lewis Carroll's original title for *Alice in Wonderland*). It fetched an amazing £15,400 at Sotheby Auction and now resides in the British Library.

Alice died in 1934, aged 82, having been the inspiration for one of the world's greatest works of fiction.

— 11 —

Turner's Cornucopia

1775-1851

When he died in 1851, Britain's greatest painter, William Turner, left a legacy of paintings that consisted of 500 oils, 2,500 watercolours and over 30,000 sketches and drawings.

His subject matter was drawn from all over the British Isles and Europe, including Venice.

However, what comes as a surprise is that Turner completed 30 watercolours of Oxford, more than any other place, even Venice.

At the time of Turner's pre-eminence the watercolour genre was the real rock and roll, particularly in its topographical form (landscape and buildings), a far superior form in technical accomplishment to oils. Today sadly this has changed, and buyers prefer oils.

Part of the reason why Oxford was so popular with Turner apart from its natural topographical appeal (the English Athens), was the fact that his mother's family lived and worked nearby in the small village of Sunningwell, four miles downstream from Oxford where they were the village butchers.

As a child Turner was a frequent visitor to the area, visiting his mother's family, and visited Oxford many times. In fact, Turner's earliest dated subject was Oxford's Folly Bridge, drawn when Turner was 12 and copied from the 1780 edition of the *Oxford Almanack*. His next view a year later produced a landscape view of the City of Oxford drawn from a hillside to the west of Oxford. These drawings were considered exceptional for a twelve-year-old as yet untutored. He was admitted to the Royal Academy Schools two years later in 1789.

Turner also attended lessons in perspective in 1790 under the tutelage of Thomas Malton, which immediately produced Turner's first drawing of buildings as their main subject, Christ Church, Tom Tower and the Cathedral taken from an unusual angle from Merton Fields.

It was also Oxford that crucially gave him his first commercial break when he was in 1799, commissioned by the prestigious *Oxford Almanack* to produce ten pieces of art work between 1799 and 1813.

The *Oxford Almanack* was first published in 1674 and included engravings and information about Oxford University and its colleges, including Heads of Colleges and a university calendar. It continues to be published to this day.

As a result of the Almanack Commission he met the great Oxford printmaker James Waterlow who commissioned him to produce two oil paintings, one of which became the iconic view down the High Street incorporating University College, Queen's College, St Mary the Virgin Church, All Saints and The Carfax and of course the famous High Street bend. It is one of the most remarkable townscapes in the history of art and eventually made the fortune of James Waterlow. It is a very popular view with artists, rivalling Venice's Rialto.

The civic authorities have even constructed a traffic island in the High Street which aids the artist greatly, being a safe place from which to draw in the middle of the road and capture all the essential elements without being run over. It is wholly appropriate that Oxford's Ashmolean Museum contains many of Turner's Works.

— 12 —

700 Years of Celibacy

1877

Once upon a time there lived a community of dons who were teachers and fellows of the Oxford Colleges. Dons were not allowed to marry and like priests lived a life of celibacy, although in all other matters lived a normal life. What is surprising is that this way of life lasted for 700 years, but for many it was an ideal environment in which to bathe in academe uninterrupted by domestic matters.

The origins of this prohibition go back to 1167 when Henry II banned English students attending the University of Paris, and Oxford was chosen as their locus academe because of the presence of so many monastic orders in the town with their ready-made Latin schools. This in fact was the origin of the colleges of Oxford University and it would seem reasonable that the monastic practices would be adopted by these fledgling colleges. Hence the ordainment of the early teachers (dons) and their vow of celibacy and consequently the ban on dons marrying.

Attempts were made from time to time to change this misogynistic way of life, but the Catholic Church and other powerful reactionary forces successfully resisted any change. The thought of don offspring disturbing the academic calm of our great seats of learning was outrageous.

However, a Liberal MP and future Prime Minister William Gladstone (Christ Church 1823-31) fought hard to have the rules changed and this he did through the Royal Commissions of 1854 and 1877.

These Royal Commissions were set up to look at the organisation of universities particularly Oxford and Cambridge which had become decadent and self-serving, and totally inefficient seats of learning where the passing of examinations was a mere formality. Entry to our once great universities was more by nepotism than academic ability.

The Royal Commissions implemented root-and-branch reforms including setting up of a powerful ruling body the Hebdomadal Council, transferring the supervision of examinations to the university and not the colleges.

Unknown Oxford

As far as the dons were concerned the 1877 Royal Commission removed all monk-like restrictions and they were allowed to marry, thus legitimising many children who had been locked away with their mothers in some modest dwelling on the outskirts of Oxford.

A whole new housing estate sprang up in North Oxford to accommodate the dons and their families. They were beautiful houses designed by the latest fashionable architects.

St John's College which owned the fields on which North Oxford was built became very rich and when the original 99-year leases expired became even more wealthy, so everybody lived happily ever after, including William Gladstone who served as UK Prime Minster on no less than four occasions for a total of 12 years and produced eight children.

Malcolm Horton

— 13 —

The One-Word Essay – The Ultimate Challenge

1914

Until recently All Souls College's one-word essay was seen as the most daunting examination in the world. It was one of the five papers candidates had to sit in an annual three-day competitive examination to select just two new Fellows from about thirty hand-picked candidates taking the exam, and if successful receive a seven-year scholarship worth £14,784 a year.

The title All Souls Fellow is one of the most glittering prizes in academe and signifies membership of one of the most exclusive clubs in the world.

All Souls, founded in 1438 by Archbishop Chichele to commemorate the dead in the Hundred Years War with France, is unique in having neither graduates nor undergraduates, just Fellows of whom there are only 80. They occupy three quadrangles of the most stunning architecture in Oxford, largely designed by Nicholas Hawksmore in the 17th century.

The one-word essay aspirants were handed an envelope which contained a slip of paper containing a single word on which candidates were required to write a three-hour essay. Over the years the words have included Originality, Water, Bias, Style, Chaos, Morality and Mercy.

Among those that have passed are Isaiah Berlin, Judge Richard Wilberforce and politicians John Redwood and William Waldegrave. The list of failures is perhaps even more awe-inspiring, including historian Hugh Trevor Roper (Lord Dacre), writer Hilaire Belloc and historian/biographer Lord David Cecil.

One of the two new fellows is permanently resident in All Souls whilst carrying out research, whilst the other known as a 'Londoner' and is required to make his way in the outside world in commerce, law, banking or politics. The 'Londoner' returns to All Souls at weekends to work on his thesis and is required to dine in Hall at least twenty-eight times per term.

The one-word essay was initiated in 1914 but scrapped in 2009 as being no longer the most suitable way of measuring the abilities of outstanding candidates. In any case the majority of the Fellows are elected by invitation; there are only fourteen examination fellows at any one time.

After the seven-year period the Examination Fellows can be re-elected annually. Some spend their whole lives in this highly exclusive environment.

Additionally, fourteen overseas academics are elected to a one-year fellowship. This was a compromise with a Royal Commission that wanted to open up All Souls to undergraduates; a prospect that would have had Archbishop Chichele turning in his grave.

An amusing observation in the *Spectator* magazine was made by the writer and Labour MP John Strachey in the 1950s, who said of the All Souls building and its inhabitants, "the birds are not worthy of the cage".

— 14 —

The Birth of The Oxford English Dictionary

1928

On 26th April 1878 James Murray, a Scottish lexicographer and philologist, was invited to a meeting of the Delegates of the Oxford University Press.

The purpose of the meeting was to explore the possibility of Murray taking on the job of editor of a new dictionary of the English Language to replace Samuel Johnson's *A Dictionary of the English Language*, published in 1755.

In 1928, fifty years after that fateful meeting with the Delegates, the Oxford English Dictionary was published, containing 414,800 word forms. Samuel Johnson's dictionary contained only 42,773 entries.

It was originally envisaged that the new dictionary would take ten years to complete but such was the complexity and scale of the work that it took 50 years to complete. It even outlived its editor-in-chief James Murray who died of pleurisy on 26th July 1915, almost certainly caused by overwork. But he had laid the foundations and it was left to his team of editors to complete the work.

Murray was a teacher at Mill Hill School when he started the work and had a scriptorium built in the grounds of the school, which consisted of a corrugated iron shed.

With such a massive project, it was soon apparent that Murray could not carry on with his teaching work and compile a dictionary. So, in 1885 he moved to Oxford, 78 Banbury Road where he built a larger scriptorium in the back garden. The post office even installed Murray's personal post box outside the house. Hundreds of slips would arrive every day from all corners of the globe and he even employed his own children to sort the slips.

The Oxford English Dictionary is being continuously updated and its second edition in printed form boasted 615,800 words. Future editions will almost certainly be published only in digitised form, being far too large to produce in printed form. The 1989 second edition ran to 20 volumes.

Other shorter versions are produced including *The Shorter Oxford English Dictionary*, which is an abridged form excluding words obsolete before 1700. *The Concise Oxford Dictionary* covers current English only. *The Pocket Oxford Dictionary of Current English* is another shorter version. All are derivatives of the complete *Oxford English Dictionary* that James Murray produced in his scriptorium from his slips of paper without the benefit of computerisation.

— 15 —

An Outbreak of Crime Writers

1925

The college dons of Oxford University have in the 20th century been responsible for an abnormal number of crime and detective novels. J.I.M Stewart (1906-1994), one of their number, who wrote under the pen name Michael Innes, wrote no less than 50 crime novels and collections of short stories. He was a Fellow at Christ Church and was a Professor of English. His most famous character was Inspector Appleby of the Yard who, under Innes' stewardship went on to become Commissioner of the Metropolitan Police.

Bruce Montgomery (1921-1978), writing under the pen name of Edmund Crispin, wrote nine novels featuring the eccentric and absent-minded amateur sleuth Gervase Fen, who is a Professor of English and a Fellow of St Christopher's College, a fictional institution located next to St John's. Bruce Montgomery graduated with a BA in Modern Languages from St John's College, having for two years been its organ scholar and choirmaster. He became a composer of some merit, his most notable work being *An Oxford Requiem* (1951). In the fifties he turned to film work, writing the scores for many British comedies including the Carry-on Series and four films in the Doctor film series. He sadly died at the early age of 57 from alcohol related problems.

Ronald Knox (1888-1957) was a theologian, a Fellow at Trinity College who wrote copiously on theological matters and was a distinguished broadcaster. He also wrote nine detective novels and short story collections featuring his private sleuth Miles Bredon.

Love Lies Bleeding
EDMUND CRISPIN
A GERVASE FEN MYSTERY

The ubiquitous J.C. Masterman (1891-1977) was a Fellow of Christ Church and University Vice Chancellor, whose wartime work as a master spymaster is featured elsewhere in this book. Sadly, he only had time to write two crime novels, both featuring a Viennese amateur sleuth named Ernest

Brendel, who was a lawyer of international fame and visited Oxford from time to time to give lectures.

Finally, Gwendoline Williams (1922-2013) was initially a writer of romantic novels who started writing detective novels in 1956. Her principal character in her 34 crime books was Inspector Coffin.

She graduated from Lady Margaret Hall, where she read History and later lectured there. Her output of romantic novels was even more prolific, 45 in total.

She wrote under two other pen names, Jennie Melville and Gwendoline Butler. However, it was as Gwendoline Williams that she received the Crime Writers' Association Silver Dagger for *A Coffin for Pandora*.

In 1949 she married Dr Lionel Butler who was a professor of Mediaeval History at the University of St Andrews and a Fellow of All Souls. They were married for 32 years and had a daughter Lucilla.

All of these distinguished dons were merely paving the way for Oxford's most illustrious detective, the world-famous Chief Inspector Morse, the brainchild of Colin Dexter OBE. But that's another story.

— 16 —

Oxford School's Air Heroes

1939-1945

Asked to name the most famous RAF pilots from the Second World War, Guy Gibson and Douglas Bader would almost certainly be on most people's list.

The fact that they were both educated at the same school, St Edward's, Oxford, is an amazing coincidence. But the school's RAF connection doesn't stop there. This impressive Victorian school situated in the leafy suburb of Summertown, North Oxford produced four other outstanding airmen.

St Edward's alma mater also include Wing Commander Adrian Warburton ("the most valuable" pilot in the RAF), Sergeant Pilot Arthur Banks, Air Commodore Louis Strange and Captain Geoffrey De Havilland, founder of the eponymous aircraft company.

The exploits of the legless pilot Group Captain Sir Douglas Bader CBE, DSO and Bar, DFC and Bar (1910-1982) are well documented in the major film classic *Reach for the Sky*, taken from Paul Brickhill's book of the same name. Early on the film highlights Bader's well known ego in a devastating crash in 1931, whilst he was carrying out some amazing and risky aerobatics, which resulted in the loss of both his legs and his discharge from the RAF.

When the Second World War broke out in 1939, equipped with his tin legs he ostentatiously applied to re-join the Royal Air Force. After overcoming initial bureaucracy ("there's nothing in regulations covering pilots with no legs") he re-joined the RAF and took part in the Battle of Britain, shooting down 22 enemy aircraft. In 1941, after baling out over German-occupied France, he spent the rest of the war in captivity, mainly in the famous Colditz Castle reserved for habitual escapees.

At the end of the war he was given the honour of leading the Victory Flypast by 300 aircraft over London.

Wing Commander Guy Gibson VC, DSO and Bar, DFC and Bar (1918-1944) came from a troubled background of parental divorce and an alcoholic mother, so his housemaster at St Edward's, A.F. (Freddie) York, and his wife became Gibson's guardians. Initially turned down by the RAF because of his short legs he went on in 1943 to lead the famous raid on the Möhne and Eder Dams, which was the subject of the blockbuster film *The Dam Busters*, for which he received the Victoria Cross. Tragically, in 1944 he was shot down whilst flying a De Havilland Mosquito over Germany by what is now thought to be a friendly fire accident by a British rear gunner who mistook his plane for a German Junker.

Wing Commander Adrian Warburton (1918-1944) DSO and Bar, DFC and two Bars, and DFC United States, having developed as the RAF's leading reconnaissance pilot added further to his reputation for his role in the defence of Malta. He played a vital role in the invasion of Sicily. His methods were risky and unorthodox, but his superiors turned a blind eye because they worked.

Such was his reputation that the United States Air Force, in the guise of Lt Col Elliott Roosevelt, the son of the President Roosevelt, requested his transfer to a USAF base in Oxfordshire, ostensibly as RAF Reconnaissance Liaison Officer. Ten days after taking up his duties, on 12th April 1944, he went missing over Munich and his remains were not discovered until 2002 in the cockpit of his plane six feet below the surface of a field just outside a small Bavarian village.

Sergeant Pilot Arthur Banks GC (1923-1944) was shot down over Northern Italy. He made contact with a partisan group and in the months that followed was their driving force. They were betrayed and captured by the Germans who tortured Banks for several days before handing him over to the Italians who tortured him further without success.

Malcolm Horton

He was stripped, doused in petrol, set alight and weighted down before being thrown into the River Po. He miraculously survived and swam to the river bank where he was recaptured and shot in the head. His captors were tried by a War Crimes Tribunal and received lengthy prison sentences. Their leader was executed. Arthur Banks remained silent throughout what was most brutal and inhuman treatment. He was awarded the George Cross posthumously and it was presented to his father by George VI.

Wing Commander Louis Strange (1891-1966) DSO, OBE, MC, DFC and Bar served as an airman in both World Wars. He was awarded the DFC and Military Cross in 1915 for carrying out one of the first tactical bombing missions. In 1940, aged 49, he returned as a pilot officer in the RAF Volunteer Reserve. He was soon on active service in France where he was awarded a Bar to his DFC. In 1944 he assisted with the planning of Operation Overlord; landing in Normandy personally liberated Chateau Lillis, repeating what he had done 24 years earlier. He was also at SHAEF Forward Headquarters in Rheims on 6-7 May 1945 to witness negotiations to the German surrender on all fronts.

He was awarded an OBE and the American Bronze Star Medal for these diplomatic services.

In 1955, the Air Council, to commemorate the enormous contribution former pupils of St Edward's made to the war effort, presented the school with a stained-glass window for the chapel depicting an unknown airman.

— 17 —

Sir John Masterman
University Don and Spymaster

1939-1945

On the face of it Sir John Masterman OBE was the stereotypical Oxford don who spent most of his life in Oxford's hallowed halls, first as a student at Worcester College where he gained a First in Modern History, a tutor at Christ Church where he was Senior Censor (a sort of welfare officer), Provost (Head) of Worcester College and then Vice-Chancellor of Oxford University. It seems inconceivable that such an establishment figure should have spent the whole of the Second World War as an MI5 spymaster. Not just any spymaster but chairman of the celebrated Twenty Committee which ran the Double Cross System of turning captured German spies into double agents working for Britain. The deal was quite simple; be executed as a spy or work for Britain as a double agent. The committee was named after the Latin XX, a typical Oxford pun.

Why should a 48-year old Oxford don volunteer for such as stressful job in the first place? The answer was guilt at not having done his bit in the First World War.

At the outbreak of the First World War in 1914 Masterman was an exchange lecturer at the University of Freiburg and as a result spent four years interned as an enemy alien. During his interment, Masterman became prolific in the German language. Unknowingly, perfect preparation for his Second World War role in MI5 20 years later. Also, Masterman was a very fit 48-year old, being a first-class sportsman excelling at cricket, hockey and lawn tennis. He reached the quarter-finals at Wimbledon twice, represented England at hockey and toured Canada with the MCC.

The job of the double agents was to feed disinformation to the Germans whilst also appearing to be carrying out effective operations for their German spymasters.

MI5 was staffed by many amateurs like himself such as commercial artists and London theatre stage carpenters. Some of their antics would have made excellent copy for the *Boy's Own Paper*! Particularly the mock destruction of the De Havilland aircraft factory, which required artists and theatre stage carpenters to give the impression from the air that the factory had been destroyed by the double cross agents, thus confirming their apparent allegiance to the Fatherland.

The Twenty Committee's most important achievement was Operation Fortitude, a plan to deceive the Germans about the location of the Normandy Landings (the D-Day Landings) which laid the foundations of Allied victory on the Western Front. So effective was the disinformation the Germans were convinced that the centre of gravity of the invasion was the Pas-de-Calais (the port on the French cost nearest England).

As a result, the Germans kept 15 divisions in reserve near Calais even after the invasion had begun 205 miles away in Normandy. So, something like 200,000 soldiers were kept ungainfully employed in Calais.

At the end of the Second World War, conscience assuaged, he returned to Oxford to continue his academic work, which included fifteen years (1946-1961) as Provost of Worcester College and a spell as Vice-Chancellor of the University of Oxford (1957-1958). In 1959 he was knighted for his services to education.

Finally, in 1972 after an 18-year battle with MI5 and the government he published in the UK a book about the work of the Double Cross System. Originally published in America in 1970, out of the reach of the Official Secrets Act, the government bowed to the inevitable and allowed publication of *The Double Cross System in the War of 1939-1945*. A lasting testimony to a truly remarkable Oxford don.

— 18 —

The Bear Inn Tie Collection

1954

The Bear Inn, situated on the junction of Blue Boar Street and Alfred Street, is internationally renowned for its ties – over 5,000 of them at the last count. Showcases of ties cover the walls and ceilings of the two bars; ties from schools, clubs, army regiments, OB associations, in fact ties from anywhere.

The collection was begun in 1954 when the landlord at the time, Alan Course, an ex-cartoonist from the *Oxford Times*, began cutting off the bottom section of customers' ties in return for a couple of pints of best bitter. The tradition has been carried on by successive landlords.

The Bear can trace its provenance back to the 13th century and has been known as Parn Hall, The Tabard, The Jolly Trooper and finally the Bear Inn. It became a coaching inn in the 18th century when it was a much larger establishment than now, having a High Street frontage.

Royal commissions and circuit judges regularly met there and in 1586 Lord Norris and his retinue were attacked at the Bear by disgruntled scholars from Magdalen as a reprisal against the imprisonment of one of their number who had stolen a deer from Shotover Royal Forest. In its prime it had over thirty rooms and stabling for thirty horses.

The Bear and, more particularly, its ties were featured in the Colin Dexter crime novel *Death is Now My Neighbour.* when Inspector Morse was trying in vain to identify a tie worn by a suspect. The landlady of the Bear identified the tie as rather prosaically being just like one she had seen on the tie rack in Marks and Spencer's.

Unknown Oxford

— 19 —

Best Council House in Britain

1959

Headington Hill Hall, situated 1½ miles from the centre of Oxford, was built in 1824 by the Morrell family, Oxford's largest brewers. It was extensively remodelled and greatly enlarged in 1858 by James Morrell Junior to designs by the architect John Thomas in the Italianate style.

The Morrell mansion boasted 51 rooms and housed 19 indoor servants and had 37 acres of landscaped gardens and parkland.

In 1953, after nearly 130 years of Morrell ownership, James Morrell III sold Headington Hill Hall to Oxford City Council. After a period of use as a rehabilitation centre it was in 1959 offered on a 21-year lease to the highest bidder.

This turned out to be a young business tycoon Robert Maxwell, or rather his company Pergamon Press, who bid £2,400 a year for a twenty-one-year lease, later extended to 75 years. Ostensibly Headington Hill Hall was to be occupied as offices by Pergamon's 400 staff; however, Maxwell somewhat deviously erected prefabricated buildings in the parkland to accommodate the staff whilst he and his family took up exclusive residence in Headington Hill Hall.

He rated it as one of his best business deals and was moved to describe it as "the best council house in the country". However, the deal coincided with his entry into politics as a prospective Labour candidate for nearby Buckingham. In answer to the questions at his adoption meeting about the suitability of a Labour candidate occupying a stately home he assured his audience that he would not be living in the hall as it was to be occupied by his employees.

Once adopted, he proceeded to spend £350,000 on restoring Headington Hill Hall and moved in with his family. Staff were kept to the confines of the prefabricated buildings although he did eventually build a proper office block.

This was a hallmark of Maxwell's approach to business: say one thing and do another.

In November 1991 in the middle of a financial crisis which forced him to sell Pergamon, Maxwell's body was found in the sea. A year later Oxford City Council negotiated a long lease with the fledgling Oxford Brooks University which is now Britain's leading new university with a student population in excess of 15,000.

From council house to a leading university, I think Robert Maxwell the Czech peasant who became an international tycoon might well have approved.

— 20 —

A Degree of Uncertainty

1963-1966

Amongst the many controversies surrounding writer Jeffrey Archer's chequered life was his claim to have graduated from Oxford University. An amazing achievement for a lad with just three 'O' levels to his name if true!

Like everything else in this brilliant huckster's life there is an element of truth garnished with great showmanship, which led to an impression of achievements way beyond the more prosaic reality.

In fact, he did spend three years at Oxford University from 1963 to 1966, the first year as a genuine student on a one-year course, the Diploma of Education (Dip Ed) in Physical Education. The other two as an interloper. The colleges were happy to allow him all the benefits of membership including representing the college at sport. In Archer's case Brasenose was the college who hosted him and, like all new students in their first week or two, he matriculated (a ceremony which admits a student to membership of Oxford University whether or not he or she eventually obtains a degree). Matriculation confers on the student lifelong membership of the university.

It is worth pausing for a moment to answer the question: how on earth did he get there in the first place?

Archer attended a minor public school, Wellington in Somerset, where he was heartily disliked by the other pupils as being cocky and boastful. Being small in stature he was bullied. Academically he was not very bright, but he did have a gift for athletics, so he went on an intense regime of bodybuilding and developed excellent body strength, allowing him to excel at not only gymnastics but also sprinting, winning the county schools 100 yards.

Despite staying on in the lower 6th for an extra three years he only managed to drag his 'O' Level passes up to three: English Literature, History and Art.

Clearly not cut out for a university education he left school and joined the army, and was even awarded a place at the Sandhurst Royal Military Academy – the elite officer training school. He lasted only three months. The universal verdict was that "he didn't fit in being universally disliked by his fellow cadets and officers alike. He was too cocky and lacked empathy."

After the army Archer spent a couple of months in San Francisco, attending a short diploma course in physical education which later transmogrified itself into a full-scale degree from the University of California.

On returning to the UK in May 1960 he joined the Metropolitan Police Force as a constable. He lasted just five months being unable to adapt to the spartan living conditions.

However, within a few months armed with his physical education 'degree' he secured the post of PE Master at Dover College, a minor public school which proved to be the key to his future development. He was a first-class PE teacher popular with the boys, and above all raising Dover College's sporting profile to the extent that it was considered to be one of the best athletic schools in the UK.

His entry into Oxford on the one-year Dip Ed course was enthusiastically supported by the Headmaster of Dover College, whose glowing reference included mention of 'A' Levels and an American university degree. All accepted by Oxford on face value. Validation procedures in those days were non-existent.

Apart from his great ability to sell himself, his greatest quality was his work ethic. Nobody worked harder than Jeffrey Archer; he was indefatigable at everything he did. In his three years in Oxford in 1960-1963 he captained the university at athletics and became President of the Oxford Athletics Union: he gained a blue as a sprinter and even represented Great Britain at 220 yards.

However, his most important role in Oxford was the work he did with Oxfam, raising its profile to become a household name, mainly through the £1m fundraising campaign where his sheer drive and energy came to the fore. He even persuaded the Beatles to support the campaign by visiting Oxford and dining in hall 'at Brasenose'.

Crucially he met his future wife Mary who was a chemistry student at St Anne's and the most brilliant student of her years, and it was not long before they were married in July 1966. He literally swept her off her feet and, despite all the trials and tribulations, they have remained married for over 50 years.

After Oxford, politics loomed and a spell in prison, and of course an enduring career as one of Britain's best-selling authors. But that's another story.

— 21 —

A Tale of Four Churches

1971

As might be expected Oxford has a Town Church and a Gown Church.

The Gown, or University Church, is St Mary the Virgin situated in the High Street just beyond All Souls and is one of Matthew Arnold's 'Dreaming Spires'. It is much beloved by artists, including J.M.W Turner when painting the famous view looking westward down the High Street incorporating the street's famous bend.

St Mary the Virgin is mentioned in Domesday although not the original church, which was largely rebuilt in the 12th and 13th centuries, although its location standing on what was the original East Gate has not.

It has been the University Church since its foundation and indeed acted as the administrative centre of the university in its early days before it had a Congregation House. St Mary's was used for meetings, ceremonies, examinations and sessions of the Chancellor's Court. It was also the place where degrees were conferred until Wren built the Sheldonian Theatre in 1669.

The Town or City Church where the mayor and corporation pray has had a variety of homes since St Martin's at the Carfax was granted by King Canute to the Benedictine monks of Abingdon in 1086. It is situated at the very western end of the High Street, beyond St Mary the Virgin, where four roads form the North, South, East and West Gates converge. The Carfax derives its name from the Latin 'quadrifurcus' – four forked.

In 1896, the body of the church was demolished in order that the road could be widened as part of the comprehensive Carfax redevelopment. However, the tower remained and is now officially the Clock Tower and Civic Belfry. The clock dates from the 17th century as do the original quarter boys (figures of men holding clubs) whose 1849 replicas strike the bells every quarter of an hour. The original quarter boys are in the Museum of Oxford, dating from the 11th century.

All Saints Church at the end of Turl Street and the High Street became the City Church in 1896, until 1971 when it seems to have been requisitioned by Lincoln College in Turl Street as its ornate new library.

What seems to have happened is that a swap occurred with St Michael's Church at Northgate, which in 1971 became the City Church. When Lincoln College was founded by the Bishop of Lincoln Richard Fleming in 1427, he settled All Saints and St Martin's Churches and livings (the rentals obtained from land and property owned in the parish given to vicar) on his new college with the power to appoint any new rector.

Therefore, Lincoln College was able to offer St Michael's in exchange for All Saints as a replacement City Church with all three livings accruing to St Michael's.

St Michael's is appropriately situated by the Cornmarket in the corn mercurial area of the city and also close to Gilbert Scott's Martyr's Memorial. St Michael's also contains the oldest stained glass in Oxford, dating from 1290.

Also, St Michael's has always had close ties with the commercial houses of Oxford which are situated in the Cornmarket area, so the City Church seems to have ended up in the most appropriate location.

— 22 —

Tortoise Racing – The Ultimate Oxford Eccentricity

1974

Until 1974 the only race associated with a tortoise was the famous children's fable involving the race with the hare – "slow and steady wins".

Then, in 1974, this philosophy was turned upside down when Corpus Christi organised the first intercollegiate tortoise race when speed became the overriding ordinance.

Oxford has always been blessed with eccentrics and eccentricities and they don't come more eccentric than university students, whilst learning to be future prime ministers and Whitehall mandarins, coming up with the idea of holding an intercollegiate tortoise race. Although not classified as a cupper, as official intercollegiate events are known, nevertheless, it produces the fiercest inter-college rivalries and controversies.

It clearly has as its inspiration the Caucus Race in *Alice in Wonderland* written by Charles Lutwidge Dodgson (Lewis Carroll), an Oxford maths tutor.

Oxford has always had a tradition of tortoise-keeping going back centuries, no doubt due to the profusion of college gardens. The earliest photograph of a college tortoise is dated 1898 and it belonged to Corpus Christi, although Trinity College records first mention a tortoise in 1785.

Since the 1970s Corpus Christi has organised an annual Tortoise Fair, the highlight of which is the Tortoise Race. This testudinal event involves placing a circle of lettuce around the college lawn, something in the order of 20 feet in diameter. The competitors with their keepers stand in the middle of the circle back to back and on the command "release", the tortoises head for the outer ring and the first reptile to reach a piece of lettuce is declared the winner.

Over the years there have been many controversies, the first being in 2003 when Balliol's reigning champion tortoise Rosa disappeared on the eve of the race. Despite headlines and appeals in the *Oxford Mail* and the best endeavours of Inspector Morse (called back from retirement), Rosa has still not been found. Trinity, next door to Balliol, was initially accused of the crime but there was no proof, apart from centuries-old antagonism between the two college. Rosa was replaced in 2007 by Matilda, a gift from a graduate of Christ Church.

In 2016 the Corpus tortoise Foxe (named after the college's founder) and Zoom of Worcester were adjudged to have drawn. So, 2017 saw the same two making the early running but Foxe was disqualified for literally biting the legs of the opposition, allowing Zoom to come through on the inside to reach the lettuce first, Emmanuelle (Regents Park) was second and Shelly of Worcester third. (Incidentally Emmanuelle is now over 115 years old.)

In 2010, Oldman, representing Corpus, won the race but the race for second and third turned into a farce when Foxe, also running for Corpus, closely trailing Oldham, developed an aversion to the lettuce, turned around and headed back to the start. This threw the race into total confusion – the Corpus keeper intervened and picked his charge up and turned him around, which incurred immediate disqualification. Christ Church complained that its tortoise Sampron had been totally disorientated by the confusion, but in the end Regents Park's Emmanuelle meandered through to claim second place, with the tiny Mercy of University College finishing third.

Despite their legendary longevity, tortoises do not live forever and both Balliol and Magdalen in 2009 suffered losses. But unwilling to surrender their place in this prestigious race, the colleges sent human representatives clearly disguised as tortoises. The human tortoises were required to eat a whole lettuce before the race and then avoid squashing the other reptilian competitors. Neither was successful, eating a whole lettuce alone being a major and unequal task.

The tortoise looms large in Oxford's legends and even received royal recognition when, in 1948, *The Times* carried a photo of the Queen, then Duchess of Edinburgh, being greeted on arrival in Oxford by the Oriel tortoise.

Interestingly, tortoises first reached British shores in the 18th century having been used as ballast on slave and whaling ships, and first appearing in Oxford in the reign of George III.

Incidentally, Oxford's eldest tortoise is Regents Park's Emmanuelle, now 115, but the oldest known tortoise in the UK was Timothy who died at the age of 160 in 2004. However, the oldest tortoise in the world is presently Jonathan, aged over 185, who lives on the Island of St Helena, where Napoleon spent his last years.

— 23 —

The Transgender Bursar

1994

Commander Simon Stone RN, 47, the Home Bursar of Exeter College, Oxford since 1988, left his office one Friday afternoon in April 1994, ostensibly at the start of a ten-day holiday with his wife and two daughters. Nine days later on the due day for his return there appeared hurrying across the front quadrangle of Exeter College; the tall figure of an elegant and attractive woman anxious to get on with her job as Home Bursar.

No, Simon Stone had not been sacked, he had merely had a transgender operation and was now officially Susan Marshall. The college and university establishment, with their usual sangfroid, didn't turn a proverbial hair. After all, this was Oxford and quite used to coping with the eccentric and bizarre personalities which had for centuries crossed its historic thresholds. Oscar Wilde, Samuel Johnson, John Betjeman, Percy Bysshe Shelley to name but a few. So, a bursar of previously good behaviour merely changing sex was not an event to get unduly excited about.

However, one woman in particular took great exception: Dame Barbara Mills, Director of the Crown Prosecution Service (1992-1998) who in March 1993 had offered Simon Stone a job as a Crown Prosecutor. Stone had ten years' experience as a naval barrister.

When Dame Barbara was told by Simon Stone that he was undergoing a sex change the job offer was completely withdrawn. On the face of it this was aberrant behaviour on her part as Dame Barbara was seen as a great promoter of women's rights. She was also an Oxonian who had attended Lady Margaret Hall, then a female-only college.

After the transgender reassignment, Susan Marshall took her case for sexual discrimination to the Employment Appeal Tribunal who found in her favour and gave her the go-ahead to take her case to an industrial tribunal.

Initially, Dame Barbara had decided to launch an appeal against the Employment Appeals judgement but on the steps of the court changed her mind and offered an out of court financial settlement to Susan Marshall, which was accepted. This was in 1998 and Marshall was by then very settled in her job as Home Bursar of Exeter.

Not everything ended happily because, not surprisingly, her marriage ended in divorce. But in 2003 Susan Marshall remarried, an event which coincided with her retirement as Home Bursar, a post she had held man and woman for 15 years with great distinction.

She also served on several key university committees and was a well-respected figure in university life. She was overall a very brave woman facing not only the controversial attitude to sex change but also taking on and winning a legal battle with the Director of the Crown Prosecution Service.

— 24 —

Morse and The Case of the Brasenose Knocker

1334

Brasenose was founded in 1509 on the site of several mediaeval halls. The most notable being Brasenose Hall from which the college acquired its name and eventually the famous bronze sanctuary knocker or brazen nose.

In 1239, Brasenose Hall first comes into history as the house of Jeffrey Jussell from whom in passed to Simon de Balindon, who in 1261 sold it to the university to form part of William Durham's settlement in University College, which in 1249 had become Oxford's first college.

This was a short-lived union because Adam Billet seized Brasenose back again for the benefit of its scholars and at this point it became a hall providing accommodation, sustenance and some teaching to its resident pupils. Brasenose settled down to its status as a hall for the next 250 years until 1509, when it became a permanent college.

The only disturbance during this period was in 1334 when it too became caught up in the riots all too common in Oxford in the 13th and 14th centuries. Only this time it was not a Town and Gown dispute but between northerners and southerners within the university. So, a migration took place to Stamford where the scholars found their own sanctuary, together with their eponymous sanctuary knocker, the Brasenose Knocker, which they had taken with them.

It must be borne in mind that at this time colleges and academic halls like churches enjoyed special privileges and once a fugitive from the law clutched the sanctuary knocker he was on immune territory and safe from the sanctions of the law.

This move to Stamford House was the third attempt by students to move away from the riots and disturbances that characterised Oxford at this time. Cambridge had been a successful migration in 1209. Northampton University in 1261, even though armed with a royal charter, was aborted after five years on the advice of bishops and magnates who feared Oxford would suffer as a result of competition from Northampton. Henry III, therefore, revoked the Royal Charter.

Stamford was an even shorter tenure. The migrants just about had time to nail the Brasenose knocker to Stamford House before Edward II, in 1334, ordered the peripatetic pupils back to Oxford. Such was their hasty departure that they forgot to bring the sanctuary knocker back with them. It was to stay firmly fixed to Stamford House for the next 600 years. During that time Stamford House had become part of Stamford School.

Then, in 1890, the college received notice from a firm of auctioneers that Stamford House was to be sold, together with its ancient knocker. The college successfully acquired Stamford House and the knocker. It was carefully examined and found to be of early 12th century origin. The knocker is the face of a lion or leopard of the type well known in heraldry. The head is brass and the ring bears dragons' heads made of iron, characteristic of English ornaments.

The original Brasenose knocker has pride of place in the Hall hanging over High Table. A replica from 1509 is to be found on the main gate.

In Colin Dexter's Inspector Morse books, the fictional Lonsdale College is frequently featured. From the author's precise geographical references

Brasenose is obviously the model. In fact, in the Carlton Television screenplays, which spawned thirty-three episodes between 1987 and 2000, Brasenose was featured in seven episodes. This perhaps is not surprising since the location's advisor for the series, Dr Philip Gasser, was the Bursar of Brasenose at the time. Like the author, in Hitchcockian style he appears in each episode, generally as a face in the crowd.

It is not generally realised that Colin Dexter is a Cambridge man, having graduated from Christ's College in 1953. A final irony, however, is that Dexter was a pupil of Stamford School and Stamford House, including the Brasenose knocker, which was part of the school until 1890 when it was returned to Oxford.

— 25 —

H. M. Postmaster General Bans College Stamps

1871

Colleges had always used a messenger service for delivering letters locally. The book-keeping involved, however, was horrendous as the charges for delivery had to be entered on the sender's battels (account for board and lodging and other expenses).

In order to save the cost of entering such trivial amounts Keble, in 1871, decided to issue its own stamps on letters or messages delivered within the centre of Oxford. The scheme was so successful that seven other colleges followed suit: All Souls, Balliol, Exeter, Hertford, Lincoln, Merton and St John's.

The first stamps bore the coat of arms and the name of the college. Each stamp also bore the name of the printer, Spier & Son, High Street, Oxford, at the foot of the stamps. Three Cambridge colleges followed suit, Queens, St John's and Selwyn.

On 28th January 1886 the Postmaster General, however, objected that the system was an infringement of the Post Office monopoly. The use of college stamps was thus curtailed. They had been in use for nearly 15 years but examples of them are rare and are much sought after by philatelists. Keble continued to use franked envelopes until the 1890s. Balliol's stamps were printed in 1885 but never used.

It would be interesting to know whether this venture into privatisation had been profitable.

— 26 —

Dames' Delight and Parson's Pleasure

1699

The River Cherwell has its source five miles south of Daventry in Northamptonshire and flows for a total of 35 miles before it joins the Thames (or Isis as it is called for its Oxford span) below Christ Church Meadow. Unlike the Isis, commercial exploitation has not been visited upon the Cherwell. It is essentially a river reserved for pleasure, being too narrow and shallow for competitive rowing. Pleasure in this instance not confined to punting or rowing but also swimming, albeit in sometimes controversial manner.

THE CHERWELL AT OXFORD

Swimming took place initially at a dammed-up pool, just below the University Parks, called Parson's Pleasure. This had been since the 17th century reserved for male bathers only and was screened from view when men took to sunbathing and bathing in the nude. This practice ceased in 1992 when

Unknown Oxford

Oxford City Council closed all of its riverside bathing places. Its site can be seen immediately to the left over the bridge by Linacre College.

Originally known as Pattern's Pleasure, it was by the 20th century generally referred to as Parson's Pleasure. The area was screened off on three sides, but the river frontage caused much embarrassment to ladies passing in their punts. To avoid such discomfort the choice was simple; they could avert their eyes or disembark just before Parson's Pleasure and walk around the area and pick up their punts again.

Naturally such a situation is a wonderful catalyst for legend and folklore. CM Bowra, the Warden of Wadham College (1938-1970) and a well-known raconteur, was with a group of other dons standing naked facing the river front when a group of ladies passed by in their punts. The other dons immediately covered their more delicate parts whereas Bowra covered his head with a towel. "My students recognise me by my face," he later explained.

The broadcaster Robert Robinson sadly wrote just one book, a hilarious piece of fiction called *Landscape with Dead Dons*. The climax in the book is when the serial killer is pursued round Oxford by the whole naked colony of Parson's Pleasure before being apprehended on the steps of the Martyrs' Memorial.

In 1934 women secured their own area close by for uninhibited bathing, called Dames' Delight. This too was screened but was closed in 1970 due to flood damage.

— 27 —

Zuleika – An Oxford Love Story

1911

A graduate of Merton College, Sir Max Beerbohm (1872-1956) was a humourist, essayist and cartoonist of international renown. He was born in London and entered Merton College in 1890 where he occupied rooms in Mob Quad until 1894. His precocious talent and anarchic wit was wonderfully in tune with the time and he began, in 1895, publishing caricatures in *The Strand* magazine and essays in the *Yellow Book*. The latter were published collectively under the somewhat facetious title *The Works of Max Beerbohm* in 1896.

However, his true masterpiece was *Zuleika Dobson*, a satirical novel published in 1911 and alternatively titled *An Oxford Love Story*. Zuleika, the eponymous heroine, decides to visit her grandfather, the Warden of Judas during Eights Week. She is so ravishing that on her arrival in Oxford as the landau rolled by sweat started to pour from the brows of the Emperors (the landmark fourteen stone heads standing in front of the Sheldonian). All the undergraduates in Oxford fall madly in love with her, including the splendid and haughty Duke of Dorset. The Duke fulfils his somewhat rash promise to lay down his life for her by drowning himself and is followed by the entire undergraduate population who plunge into the Isis like lemmings with great cries of "Zuleika". That evening Zuleika asks her maid to consult Bradshaw to see if it is possible to go direct from here to Cambridge!

Max Beerbohm was knighted in 1939, although from 1910, at the time of his marriage, he lived mainly in Italy. He returned home during the two world wars and established a reputation as a broadcaster.

According to the distinguished Oxford academic Lord David Cecil (1902-1986), Beerbohm was "the finest expression of the comic spirit produced by any English writer in the 20th century".

Interestingly, in 1952 Beerbohm gave permission for Sir Osbert Lancaster to paint twelve scenes from his *Zuleika* novel for the Randolph Hotel. He even suggested which scenes might be chosen and hoped that the poor Emperors heads would not be ignored. They were not. The pictures still hang in the hotel in the Lancaster Suite, which is now used mainly for afternoon teas.

Osbert Lancaster (1908-1986) like Beerbohm attended Charterhouse School and Oxford; he was an alumnus of Lincoln College. He was a cartoonist, historian, stage designer, architect and author. He was probably most famous for his daily cartoon in the *Daily Express*, which ran from 1938 until 1981, his most notable character being Maudie Littlehampton.

Malcolm Horton

— 28 —

The Hell Raiser from the Valleys

1944

In February 1966 Richard Burton and Elizabeth Taylor appeared at the Oxford Playhouse in a student production of Marlowe's *Dr Faustus*.

The aim of such a star-spangled production was to raise money for an extension to the playhouse to house a new acting studio.

It seemed as though the whole world's media resources had been switched to Oxford to cover the event.

Burton and Taylor at this time were probably the most famous people on the planet having just completed the most expensive movie of all time, *Cleopatra*, which in today's terms would have cost £500m, with Elizabeth Taylor picking up a cool £50m for her starring part in the film. In addition, they had not long been married. They were the Posh and Becks of their day but even more so.

The question constantly being asked was why the two most sought-after actors of their day were giving up time to perform for nothing in an Oxford University Students production of *Dr Faustus*.

The answer came as a great surprise to the world at large. It was Richard's way of repaying a twenty-year debt to Neville Coghill, the show's director. He was the playhouse's producer and director and in 1944 had given Burton his first big break at the same venue in a student production of Shakespeare *Measure for Measure*, which effectively launched his career. He was a member of Exeter College reading English Literature and Coghill was his tutor.

Then the larger question now loomed: how on earth did this hellraising, hard drinking maverick from the South Wale mines, the twelfth child of a hard-drinking miner, manage to lift himself out of the black bowls of the mines to attend what was in those days the province of the privileged and wealthy? The dreaming spires of Oxford was no place for such an obviously proletarian misfit.

Oxford would soon send him packing back to where he belonged. In fact, the opposite was the reality, he literally took Oxford by storm: like some Viking invader returning from an earlier age to terrorise Oxford once again.

Richard Burton's birth name was Richard Walter Jenkins, the same as his father. He was born on 10th November 1925, the twelfth of thirteen children born to Richard and Edith Jenkins. Sadly, two years later after giving birth to the thirteenth child, Edith died.

Due to circumstances at home a widower father who had a tendency to drink (he was a 12 pint a day man and who was often away for weeks on end on booze cruises round the local pubs), Richard was brought up by his sister Cecilia and her husband Elfed. Cis as he affectionately referred to her was effectively his mother for 15 years.

Richard was a very bright boy, possessing many talents both academic and sporting. He was an avid reader of literature and poetry whilst at the same time being a first-rate rugby player and captain of the school cricket team. He was also a very good boxer. He had a fine voice and won the Eisteddfod as a soprano. He had a gift for acting and as time went on his voice developed the fine mellifluous baritone for which he was immediately recognisable.

Several school teachers recognised his talents and took a special interest in him. One Philip Burton was a bit of a thespian who produced and wrote plays for the BBC. Richard moved in with Philip Burton to further this nurturing of his talents, particularly acting, and he even changed his name by deed pole from Jenkins to Burton.

Richard passed the eleven plus scholarship to attend Neath Secondary School where he went on to achieve exceptional results in the School Certificate.

He had already joined the local drama group and starred as Professor Higgins in *Pygmalion* in the school play. He also joined Squadron 499 of the Air Training Corps Section of the Royal Air Force, which was commanded by his adoptive father Philip Burton.

Armed with his school certificate, Richard with Philip's help applied for an RAF Scholarship at Exeter College Oxford. These six-monthly scholarships were awarded to appropriately qualified cadets prior to active service in the RAF as prospective pilots and navigators.

His performance in *Pygmalion* had come to the attention of the dramatist Emlyn Williams, who in 1963 offered him a part in his new play *Druid's Rest*, which premiered at the Royal Court, Liverpool before moving to London's West End to the St Martins' Theatre. Richard received very favourable reviews from *The New Statesman*; a remarkable beginning for a boy still at school.

Then it was off to Oxford which would change his life forever.

He arrived in Oxford and immediately made friends with the actor Robert Hardy who was reputed to be 20th in line to the throne. Hardy was in thrall to Richard: "I had never met anyone like him before nor have I since." He was genuinely a great man, a leader who had so much 'size' and originality. A leader among leaders, the principal hell raiser amongst hell raisers (he breathed the very air of danger). Hardy recalls that they all drank but Richard out drank us all. It led one night to a jealous rival spiking his beer with wood alcohol, after Burton had sunk a sconce (two pints) in ten seconds. He collapsed down the stairs and damaged his back.

He managed to accomplish his RAF work with ease and excelled at his English & Italian Studies. When he left to join the RAF, he was one of 12 prize winning cadets.

"This boy is a genius and will be a great actor. He is outstandingly handsome and robust, very masculine with deep inward fire." This was the judgement of Neville Coghill, Fellow in English Literature and Director of the Friends of Oxford University Dramatic Society and the man who gave Burton the lead in *Measure for Measure*. The performance was watched by several West End luminaries (Gielgud, Rattigan and Binkie Beaumont).

Oxford remained a beacon throughout his life and Burton did at one time consider becoming a Fellow of St Peter's College and teaching.

The only disappointment was the RAF turning him down as a pilot due to his poor eyesight; he became a navigator instead. In any case the war came to an abrupt end before Burton completed his training

Once demobbed he looked up Binkie Beaumont, the West End impresario, who immediately put him under contract and the rest is history as they say.

The one enemy he didn't manage to defeat was alcohol and he died at the tragically young age of 58.

— 29 —

Light of the World

1854

As well as the artistic treasurers contained in its public museums and galleries such as the Ashmoleum, Oxford's colleges are veritable art galleries which are the envy of most municipal galleries.

Their collections of sculptures, paintings, wood carvings and stained glass are priceless and are generally accessible to the public.

Keble College's 'The Light of the World' by Holman Hunt (1827-1910) is the most famous work of art possessed by any college.

Like Keble itself, founded in 1868, it has been surrounded by controversy since it was first conceived.

Keble College architecturally is unlike any other college in Oxford; its architect William Butterfield's idiosyncratic use of bricks of different colours creates elaborate patterns and illusions. He even sunk the lawn to give his buildings an increased sense of height. You either love or hate it. John Betjeman loved it.

The 'Light of the World' painting was not specially commissioned for Keble College's imposing chapel. The original painting, 'Light of the World', was begun in 1849 and took four years to complete; the medium being oil on canvas. It was conceived 20 years before Keble College became the flagship of the Oxford Movement. Hunt actually produced his iconic painting in furtherance of his pre-Raphaelite ideals and moved the art critic and social historian John Ruskin to state that 'Light of the World' "was one of the very noblest works of sacred art produced in this or any other age."

It is supposed to depict the following words: "Behold I stand at the door and knock. If any man hear my voice and open the door. I shall come in to him and will sup with him and he with me."

Hunt was a founder member of the pre-Raphaelite Brotherhood along with John Everett Millais and Dante Gabriel Rossetti and twelve others. Their aim was to revitalise art by detailed observation of the natural world in a spirit of religious devotion rejected by the mechanistic approach by artists such as Raphael and indeed the founder of the Royal Academy, Sir Joshua Reynolds.

'The Light of the World' was exhibited at the 1854 Summer Exhibition and was an immediate hit with the public. It was purchased by Thomas Combe, Superintendent of the Clarendon Press, the university printers, for £400. He was a patron of the pre-Raphaelite Brotherhood and purchased many of their paintings. On his death in 1872 his widow Martha gave 'The Light of The World' to Keble on the understanding that it would be housed in the chapel. The college's architect, William Butterfield, rejected the idea and it was displayed in the library. It was moved to its present position only after the construction in 1892 by another architect, J.T. Micklethwait, of the side chapel to accommodate it, where it can be viewed today.

No doubt, because of the financial exigencies imposed by the building of the new side chapel, the college authorities charged the public a fee to view the painting. This did not please Hunt and out of ire he painted a larger, life-size version between 1900-1904. However, because of failing eyesight he was assisted by the English painter Edward Hughes.

It was purchased by the ship owner and social reformer Charles Booth who immediately sent the painting on a world tour. It was claimed that four fifths of the Australian population viewed the painting. On its return from Australia it was hung in St Paul's Cathedral, where it can be seen in the cathedral's Middlesex Chapel.

There is a third smaller version of 'Light of the World', painted in pastels between 1851-1856 that is on display in the Manchester City Art Gallery, which purchased it in 1964. Engraved reproductions were widely hung in nurseries, schools and church buildings.

It even inspired Arthur Sullivan's 1873 oratorio 'Light of the World', which was received with great critical acclaim but suffered by comparison to the Gilbert & Sullivan operas which were just emerging to immense public acclaim.

Interestingly, the models used in the original painting for the head of Christ were the poet Christina Rossetti, wife of Dante Rossetti, and her sister-in-law, the artist and poet Elizabeth Siddal.

Holman Hunt was married twice, once to Fanny Waugh who died in childbirth and her sister Edith. It was illegal at the time in Britain to marry one's deceased wife's sister, so he lived mostly in Italy.

In 1905, he was appointed to the Order of Merit by King Edward VII.

— 30 —

Beaumont Palace – Birthplace of Richard Coeur de Lion

1131

The Normans were prolific castle builders; around 1,000 castles were built in the Middle Ages in order to consolidate their conquests in England and Wales.

Royal Palaces were not a priority but the one palace that stands out is the Conqueror's Tower of London, which was also a castle.

One of the few other Royal Palaces built during the Norman period was Henry I's (The Conqueror's fourth son) Beaumont Palace in Oxford, constructed in 1130.

Its primary purpose was to provide comfortable accommodation whilst the royals and their friends were visiting the nearby Woodstock Hunting Park, which had also been popular with the later Anglo-Saxon kings, including Alfred the Great.

Originally known as the King's House, Beaumont Palace was located just outside the North Gate in Oxford, roughly on the corner of what is now Beaumont Street and Walton Street, opposite Worcester College.

Henry II and his Queen Eleanor of Aquitaine visited Beaumont Palace frequently and two of their sons Richard Coeur de Lion in 1157 and John in 1167.

However, Henry II's interest was hunting not deer or boar but a beautiful woman, The Fair Rosamund. He had installed her at Woodstock in the Hunting Lodge, which he upgraded to a palace and when in Oxford he lived at Woodstock with Rosamund as man and wife with Queen Eleanor safely housed eight miles down the road in Beaumont Palace.

After Queen Eleanor's death in 1204 Beaumont Palace became much less used by the royals and in 1275 Edward I granted the palace to a succession of royal emissaries and relations. In 1304, the dismantling of the palace began when the Sheriffs of Oxford were allowed to remove stone and timber for repairs to Oxford Castle. In 1318, the remaining buildings were granted by Edward II to the Carmelite Friars in return for their prayers for a safe escape from Bannockburn where he had been heavily defeated by Robert Bruce.

The Carmelites occupied what was left of Beaumont Palace until 1538 at which time they became victims of Henry VIII's Reformation and were forced to disband. The palace was largely dismantled, the stone and timber being used for building Henry VIII's new college of Christ Church.

What little remained of the palace was destroyed in the laying out of Beaumont Street in 1829. However, the 12th century arch and nook shafts found their way to North Oxford, which was at this time being developed as a residential area.

The arch became a sort of garden feature in one of the grander houses built in North Oxford called The Avenue, 302 Woodstock Road, the property of the building developer George Kimber.

All that remains of the original Beaumont Palace site is a stone tablet set in a pillar with the inscription, "Near to this site stood King's House later known as Beaumont Palace".

With the university dons being allowed to marry in the 1877 University Reforms, North Oxford was developed to house the dons and their families.

Malcolm Horton

In 1965 some of the original North Oxford houses were pulled down to make way for the Bishop Kirk School. This in turn was demolished to make way for a new housing development in 1994. At this time the Carmelites had a house in Osberton Road adjacent to 302 Woodstock Road; this too was demolished to make way for a housing development.

The Carmelites moved to Boars Hill to a large house and estate owned by the family of the Poet Laureate Robert Bridges. This is now being used as a retreat.

At the same time as the move to Boars Hill, what remained of the Beaumont Palace Arch found its way to Boars Hill. Today the remains can be seen just behind the imposing house. Sadly, they only amount to a disorderly pile of stones, like a set of jigsaw pieces waiting to be assembled. The pillars at the entrance to the retreat are thought to have come from the arch as well.

Although not of great substance these rather forlorn remains are the oldest architectural relics in Oxford along with Oxford Castle.

— 31 —

John Deydras – Oxford's Pretender to the Throne

1318

British history is littered with pretenders to the throne, well known and not so well known, the most famous being Charles II, Bonnie Prince Charlie, Lambert Simnel and Perkin Warbeck.

But one more humble pretender, John Deydras of Oxford, has largely been forgotten by history. In 1318 he turned up at Beaumont Palace in Oxford and announced that he was the legitimate monarch. Edward II was not at home at the time but summoned him to Northampton where parliament was being held.

The basis of Deydras' claim was that he looked remarkably like Edward I, tall and good looking but minus one ear. And this was the root of the problem.

He insisted that when a child a royal nurse was neglectful in her duties and left him unattended in the castle yard and a pig bit his ear off. The nurse, knowing she would be in serious trouble swapped the one-eared child for a carter's baby who looked remarkably like John Deydras but with one important difference, he had two ears. Whilst the carter's baby grew up to become Edward II, Deydras had grown up in poverty.

At the time this story did not sound quite as preposterous as it clearly was because Edward II was a very unpopular king seeming to possess none of the virtues of a true monarch. He was not statesmanlike, had just lost Scotland in the Battle of Bannockburn, was forever quarrelling with the noblemen who bankrolled him and had plebeian hobbies and tastes. He much preferred the company of peasants to lords. He abhorred monarchical activities, preferring such lower-class pursuits as ditch digging and thatching. Above all he was homosexual and was obsessed by his great favourite Piers Gavaston, who he granted lands and titles to, much to the disgust of his jealous noblemen who in 1312 had Gavaston murdered. On the face of it therefore, there seemed to be some basis for the claim. Deydras challenged Edward to a duel and as a result was taken before Edward at Northampton where the Parliament of 1318 was being held.

Edward greeted his potential usurper with the words "Welcome my brother". Edward seems to have taken the whole affair as a huge joke and wanted to make Deydras a court jester. However, Edward's barons and his wife Isabella wanted Deydras put on trial for sedition. During cross examination Deydras finally admitted that his story was untrue, claiming his pet cat was the devil in disguise and had led him astray one day while he was walking across Christ Church Meadow.

He was found guilty as charged and both he and his cat (just to be on the safe side) were hanged and Deydras' body burnt.

However, the whole affair put doubts into Isabella's mind after all her husband's erratic behaviour and plebeian tastes, which were not those of a true born monarch.

His predilection for male lovers and his neglect of her. His later lover Hugh Despenser even had her children taken away from her. It was no wonder she took a lover, Roger Mortimer, and these two in 1327 had Edward murdered in the most gruesome way (a hot poker inserted up his rectum). As Edward was so unpopular at that time nobody turned a hair; relieved to be rid of a burden on the kingdom.

Maybe Deydras and his cat did change the course of history; they seem to have been the final straw as far as Queen Isabella was concerned.

— 32 —

Summer Is a Coming In

1500

"Summer is a coming in
Loudly Sing Cuckoo
Grows the seed and blows the mead
And spring the wood anew
Sing Cuckoo."

May Day is an ancient Northern Hemisphere spring festival and holiday thought to have originated during the days of the Roman Empire.

The celebration of the springtime fertility of the soil and livestock meant that farm labourers, having completed their parturition duties, were given a day off to enjoy the traditional May Day customs.

These included dancing round a maypole, Morris dancing and the crowning of a May Queen, customs that dated back to Anglo-Saxon times.

Oxford, however, had its own unique way of celebrating May Day mornings, featuring Magdalen College Tower.

At 6am, the college choristers climb the 172 steps to the top of the college's Great Tower and proceed to welcome the rising sun with the singing of an invocation to the summer, *Hymn us Euchroites*, composed by Benjamin Rogers in 1685 although the choral welcome dates back to the early 16th century.

A large crowd gathers along the High Street just outside the West Gate, and across Magdalen Bridge to listen to the choir sing its seasonal welcome to the summer followed by the singing of traditional madrigals, bell ringing and Morris dancing.

Many of the students assembled below have been up all night attending May Balls, dressed in formal-looking attire and somewhat worse for wear after an evening of revelry.

Since the 1960s there has been a tradition of jumping into the River Cherwell flowing beneath Magdalen Bridge. Unfortunately, such exploits have led to serious injuries due to the shallowness of the water under the bridge.

The revelling and festivities continue all down the High Street to Radcliffe Square where the Morris dancers are in full swing. Other college chapels join in the madrigals and traditional songs.

Holman Hunt's 1890 painting of May Morning on top of Magdalen Tower helped popularise the event and people from all over the world gather on Magdalen Bridge and the High Street on a May morning, no longer being bombarded by eggs and flour from students on the tower as they were in the 18th century.

Malcolm Horton

— 33 —

Religious Turmoil Creates Martyrs and Leaves 400 Dead

1589

One of Oxford's most famous landmarks is architect Sir George Gilbert Scott's Martyrs' Memorial, completed in 1843. Located at the beginning of Saint Giles Street it commemorates three Protestant bishops, Latimer, Ridley and Archbishop Crammer being burnt at the stake in Broad Street in 1555 and 1556 for refusing to renounce the Protestant faith. The memorial is sited in St Giles Street and not Broad Street because the former is in a more prominent position. (This story is well known to any who have been on a conducted tour of Oxford.) However, that is only one side of the story, so to speak.

Indeed, much historical significance is given to the events because it was Catholic Mary I's revenge for the momentous events surrounding her father Henry VIII's Reformation of 1534 when he broke with Rome and established the Church of England, seemingly as a means of casting aside Mary's mother Queen Catharine of Aragon in favour of Anne Boleyn. Altogether, more than 300 Protestants perished at the stake during Queen Mary's short reign (1553-1558). Hence her sobriquet, Bloody Mary.

It is largely overlooked by guides that less than a mile from Saint Giles at the end of Holywell Street, there is a more modest memorial, erected in 2008 on the nearest house in Holywell Street to the Holywell Gallows where, in 1589, four Roman Catholics were executed for their Catholic faith, during the reign of the Protestant 'Good Queen Bess' (Elizabeth I), Bloody Mary's sister. In fact, over 100 Roman Catholics were executed during her long reign and, as from 1589, Roman Catholics were barred from attending the university for nearly 300 years, not being allowed back until 1872.

To return to our four Roman Catholic martyrs, two were priests, George Nichols and Richard Yaxley, and the other two were worshipers, Thomas Belson and Humphrey Pritchard. The priests were convicted of treason and hung, drawn and quartered. The laymen for felony and merely hung. The priests' heads were displayed at Oxford Castle and their quarters were hung on the four city gates.

George Nichols was a native of Oxford who was educated at Brasenose College where he obtained a BA degree in 1571. He went to Dovai College in Rheims and was ordained as a Catholic priest in 1583. He was sent back to Oxford to undertake his rather dangerous mission. He converted many in Oxford to the Catholic faith including a convicted highwayman. In 1589 he was arrested at the Catherine Wheel hostelry which was being used to hold an illegal Roman Catholic service. Richard Yaxley, Thomas Belson and Humphrey Pritchard were all arrested at the same service.

However, by far the most famous Catholic martyr was St Edmund Campion who was one of the first graduates from the newly-founded St John's College. In 1569, he was made a Deacon in the Church of England. He became the most popular man of the university and as a result was chosen to welcome Queen Elizabeth on her visit to Oxford in 1566. She was extremely impressed. Suspected of leaning towards Rome, and fearing arrest, he escaped to Dovai in Rheims and in 1573 joined the Society of Jesus in Bohemia and became Professor of Rhetoric at Prague University.

In 1580, after an absence of over 10 years, he returned to England on a Jesuit mission. It was a very high-profile mission and he upset his Anglican opponents. In July 1581 he was caught in Wantage and sent up to London. He was tried on a charge of conspiracy, found guilty and hanged.

In 1987, George Nichols and the other three arrested at the Catherine Wheel were beautified (entrance into Heaven) by Pope John Paul II. Edmund Campion was canonised (made a saint) by Pope Paul VI in 1970.

— 34 —

Christchurch Time and Great Tom – Oxford's Largest Bell

1680

At five past nine every night, Christ Church's Great Tom Bell tolls 101 times to alert the students that the college gates were closing for the night. The figure of 101 was the student population of the college in 1546 at the time of the college's foundation. To be precise, 100, the other one was added in 1682 when Christopher Wren added the magnificent Tom Tower by which time the student population had increased by 1 since 1546.

The seemingly odd time of 9:05pm was 9:00pm local time. That was until the advent of the railways in the 19th century. Until then, every town and village functioned on their own time which was later than Greenwich time the further west you travelled. Bristol for instance was 13 minutes behind Greenwich time. Oxford was five minutes behind Greenwich.

The advent of the railway time tables and telegraph meant the standardisation of time in the UK at least, although this was probably not well received by Horologists.

Perversely, Oxford still retains a remnant of the old system with the Christ Church curfew and also in relation to lecture times which always start at five past the hour; probably quite useful when you're an overhung student.

Looking down St Aldates from Carfax the looming presence of Sir Christopher Wren's ogee-topped Tom Tower dominates the skyline. The eponymous tower was designed in 1682 to house Christ Church's massive bell, Great Tom, which weighs just under 7 tons and is seven feet in diameter. It originates from Osney Abbey, where it was the largest of the eight bells that were transported up to Christ Church in 1546 to the newly designated cathedral of St Frideswide.

In 1542, Henry VIII decided to create the new See of Oxford, which until then had been part of Lincoln. He chose as his new cathedral the 12th century

Osney Abbey which was located roughly where Oxford railway station is today. Then in 1546 he moved the cathedral to St Frideswide which had already been appropriated as the college chapel for his newly-opened college of Christ Church. This was a rationalisation in line with his policy of suppressing the monasteries. He was thus able to close Osney Abbey and remove its treasures. Osney's bells were installed in St Frideswide's tower, except the largest, Great Tom, which was put on one side for a special project.

Cardinal Wolsey had begun Christ Church in 1525; it was to be called Cardinal College and he asset stripped twenty-two monasteries to provide funds for his new college which was to be the grandest in all Oxford.

Perhaps because it was Oxford's 13th foundation it was inevitable that Wolsey should fall from grace, having incurred Henry VIII's displeasure for his extravagant use of power. Although Ann Boleyn may also have been influential in Wolsey's demise! Henry sacked Wolsey in 1529 and took over and finished the new college, renaming it Christ Church in 1546.

Wolsey had been planning a new chapel for the college and had already demolished three bays of St Frideswide Priory and it is for this reason that Oxford has the smallest cathedral in England, although it now has the largest diocese.

At some point in Mary Tudor's short reign (1553-1558), Great Tom was renamed Mary in honour of the new monarch. But by the beginning of the 17th century, Great Tom, no longer Mary, was not a happy bell and was recast no fewer than four times before it was finally bought up to scratch by Christopher Hodson, a London founder who also made three new bells for St Frideswide.

In 1680, ten bells were rehung in the cathedral tower with Tom set aside for a new home. This new home was Christopher Wren's Tom Tower – where it has resided since 1688. It is not only Oxford's largest bell but also its loudest, so it doesn't ring again after curfew at 9:05pm until 8:00am the next morning.

Tom Tower had a clock installed from the very beginning and, when examined by clockmakers T Cook & Sons in 1886 with a view to effecting repairs, it was decided that it was not worth repairing. However, its dials, dial work and hammer work were all in good condition and a new clock incorporating these existing parts could be made for £300. It was also decided not to run the clock by electricity.

Since its final recasting in 1688 Great Tom seems to have been a happy bell falling silent only for the duration of the First and Second World Wars.

— 35 —

Elias Ashmole – Controversial Founder of Ashmolean Museum

1683

In 1683, Elias Ashmole founded the eponymous Ashmolean Museum, Britain's first public museum and the first university museum in the world.

He offered to donate his collection of 'rarities' to Oxford University provided they built a suitable museum in which the collection could be displayed.

The university readily agreed, and a fine building arose on a site next to the Sheldonian Theatre in Broad Street, designed by Thomas Wood, a local stonemason.

Ashmole had obtained his collection of 'rarities' from the Tradescant family under somewhat dubious and controversial circumstances, which highlighted the ruthless and buccaneering nature of his personality.

But due credit must be given to the Tradescants who had assembled this remarkable collection of rarities.

John Tradescant the elder was a gardener, no ordinary gardener for he was keeper of His Majesty's Garden Vines and Silkworms in Stuart times. In his endeavours to procure exotic plants and blooms he travelled throughout Europe and the Far East. Being of a curious nature he collected anything natural, manmade and exotic that the world could offer.

He soon built up a sizable collection of 'curiosities', which he augmented by dealings with other collectors and travellers. His collection became knowns as Tradescant's Rarities and Curiosities. His son John the younger carried on his father's good work and he even travelled to the 'New World' Virginia where he famously obtained the cloak of the Indian Chief Powatan, the father of Pocahontas.

Other items in the Tradescant collection included the last dodo from Mauritius, a mummy's hand, a mermaid's heart, crocodile eggs, lions' teeth, and a sliver of wood from the True Cross.

The Tradescant collection of rarities and curiosities became known as the Ark and John Tradescant the younger allowed the public to view the collection at his house in Lambeth.

Then, in 1680, onto the scene came the opportunistic Elias Ashmole, an entrepreneur and man of many parts. His main claim to fame was the authorship of a book entitled *History of the Order of the Garter*. His interests included astrology alchemy, magic and antiquarianism and he was able to pursue these by virtue of being, in 1644, appointed the Commissioner for Excise, which meant coming to Oxford which was the Royalist capital during the Civil War. He even entered Brasenose College and studied mathematics and physics although he did not stay long enough to take a degree. After leaving Lichfield Grammar School he had qualified as a solicitor in 1638. His other great 'preoccupations' were fortune hunting and social climbing. His first marriage was the latter, Eleanor Mainwaring, who was from the aristocracy but impecunious. She died in childbirth when only 20. He didn't make the same mistake with his second marriage; he concentrated on wealthy older widows and in fact proposed to three simultaneously. The one he married, Lady Mary Mainwaring, was immensely rich as a result of three advantageous marriages where the husband in each case died on her. Elias and Lady Mainwaring were married much against the wishes of her family, who recognised his less than altruistic ambition.

Within a few years the marriage broke down and Mary sued for divorce. Elias kept the lion's share of her wealth as was the custom in those days when on marriage a woman's assets automatically passed to the husband. He was thus able to live the life of a gentleman and pursue his interests at leisure.

One of his interests or obsessions became the Tradescant Rarities. According to John Tradescant the younger's wife Hester, Elias Ashmole got her husband drunk and persuaded him to will the collection of rarities to Ashmole, leaving her with just a lifetime interest. John Tradescant died of natural causes and Elias harassed Hester, even moving into the house next door from where he could more easily keep an eye on the collection of rarities. All was solved when Hester was found dead face down in the garden pond. Unfortunately, Inspector Morse was not around at the time.

The way was now free for Elias to go ahead with his long-held ambition of setting up The Ashmoleum Museum and a place in the history books.

The Ashmoleum Museum remained in Broad Street until 1845 when it moved to a much grander location in Beaumont Street opposite the Randolph Hotel. The Old Ashmoleum now houses the Museum of the History of Science.

— 36 —

Cecil Rhodes – Controversial Imperialist

1902

Oriel College's Rhodes Building commemorates one of Oxford's most influential graduates and patrons, Cecil Rhodes (1853-1902), the fifth son of the vicar of Bishop's Stortford in Hertfordshire. It took him eight years to obtain his degree at Oriel due to the fact that, not long after coming up in 1874, he was diagnosed as being terminally ill. As a result, he returned to South Africa where he had spent a short period prior to going up to Oxford, assisting his elder brother in running a cotton growing business in Natal, from which he made a small fortune.

In the warmer climate, his health improved significantly, and he returned to Oxford where, at the age of twenty-eight, he obtained his degree.

He returned to South Africa and made a huge fortune from mining diamonds and other business activities. He became Prime Minister of the Cape Colony from 1890-1896. Such was his importance in the region that Rhodesia was named after him.

Throughout his lifetime he supported his alma mater Oriel College with regular financial donations and on his death in 1902 left the college £100,000 (equivalent of £12m in 2019).

The college showed its gratitude by erecting the Rhodes Building on the High with his statue set in a niche at first floor level. The Rhodes Building was supposed to be the new college entrance. It never caught on as students preferred the old Oriel Square entrance.

He was a fervent believer in the British Empire and the largely Oxford educated men who administered it. In order to spread the expertise and leadership qualities needed he introduced The Rhodes Scholarships to be awarded to men from the Old Empire, America and Germany.

America and Germany were included because he felt they were key to securing peace in the world. Two world wars shattered that objective and meant withdrawing scholarships to Germans for the duration of those conflicts.

The Rhodes Trust was set up to administer the Scholarship and a fine new headquarters, Rhodes House, was built to a design by Basil Champneys.

Academic achievements were not to be the criterion for the scholarship, as a love of sport and leadership potential were also to be rewarded. Recipients include former American President Bill Clinton; Dom Mintoff, former Prime Minister of Malta; Norman Manley, former Prime Minster of Jamaica; James Fulbright, founder of Fulbright Scholarships; and the American writer Edward de Bono. Cecil Rhodes was undoubtedly a colonialist, racist and anti-feminist.

There were no scholarships for women in his lifetime. Since his death females have been included as recipients of The Rhodes Scholarships. Also, the catchment area for scholarships has been widened to include the whole world. Particular emphasis is given to selecting men and women with the necessary attributes to lead their countries.

Retrospectively, he has been much criticised for his imperialist dogma, anti-feminism and colonial exploitation of the local population as cheap labour, but it must be remembered that he was very much a man of his time when such attitudes were de rigueur and pulling down his statue won't change history. Rather it's a reminder of the less savoury aspects of Britain colonial exploration of the old empire and its native populations.

However, his lasting legacy will be his Rhodes Scholarships of which there are 100 awarded each year. The largest number, 32, still go to the United States with only two going to Germany; the rest are students from Commonwealth countries.

He never married and was almost certainly a homosexual who was in love with his private secretary Neville Pickering. Pickering died of septicaemia, to be followed in 1902 by Cecil Rhodes who died from heart failure aged only 48.

— 37 —

Gaudy Night – A Convivial Return

Oxford colleges are famous for their social gatherings of former students (members) and none more so than The Gaudy, made famous by Dorothy L Sayers in her novel, *Gaudy Night*.

It features Lord Peter Wimsey who is a guest of Helen Vane when attending a gaudy at her alma mater Somerville College.

The word gaudy or gaude comes from the Latin word gaudere meaning to rejoice. It was used from the Elizabethan period to describe the freshmen dinner but by the 17th century it had a wider usage, covering any college commemorative feast.

Such gaudies are now widespread throughout the colleges and give alumni or old members an opportunity to return to their college to spend a convivial evening eating and drinking. They are usually arranged in year groups so that contemporaries can meet again. The time interval between such gaudy nights is seven to ten years and they are held in both winter and summer.

New College has adopted the spelling gaude and arranges for a section of the college's world-famous choir to stand on the steps leading up to the Hall to sing a summons. The members make their way round the Great Quad to listen, before proceeding up the steps and into the Hall, where a sumptuous dinner awaits, accompanied by a plentiful supply of liquid refreshment.

In recent years the spirit of the gaudy has been extended to the 'other place', Cambridge, where the majority of the Oxford colleges have twinned with a college on the basis of some common denominator such as year of foundation or names in common. They are known as sister colleges and college members attend special dinners and other social events in Oxford and Cambridge.

— 38 —

The Black Assizes at Oxford Castle

1577

The late 16th century was a period of religious turmoil with the sectarian pendulum swinging backwards and forwards from Protestant to Catholic and back again as the English crown passed from Henry VIII's children Edward VI, Mary I and Elizabeth I.

The vengeances wreaked at each change were terrifying with hundreds burning at the stake or being executed in other ways. The most famous act of corporal punishment was the burning at the stake in Broad Street of the three Oxford Martyrs, Protestant Bishops Latimer, Ridley and Archbishop Cranmer. This was Mary I's (Bloody Mary) most infamous act of retribution for her father's treatment of her Catholic mother, Catherine of Aragon.

One of the victims for a fairly minor offence was Rowland Jenkes, "a saucy foul-mouthed Catholic bookseller", who was tried at the Oxford Assizes on 6th July 1577 for uttering a treasonable word against Queen Elizabeth (but really for selling Catholic literature). He was sentenced to have his ears nailed to the pillory with liberty to cut himself free. Feeling somewhat aggrieved at the prospect of losing his ears he responded by laying a curse on the court and city.

At that time the Assizes were held in the Shire Hall of Oxford Castle which also housed the jail. It was a hot summer's day and the stench of the prisoners was quite overwhelming. Within 40 days over 300 people died of gaol fever, which developed over the course of the trial from the stench of the prisoners.

The victims included the Lord Chief Baron (Senior Judge), Sir Henry Bell, the High Sheriff Sir Richard Douly, the lessor barons, court officials, the entire jury and nearly 300 spectators. Rowland Jenkes and all the other prisoners were not affected and rather curiously no women or children died.

Some years later a manuscript came to light which attributed the deaths to mass poisoning, perpetrated by Rowland Jenkes.

It would seem that Jenkes, while in custody awaiting trial, was allowed in the company of a prison officer, liberty to walk around Oxford. During his peregrinations he somehow persuaded an apothecary to make up a prescription of deadly poison which he convinced the prison officer and apothecary was to kill rats that were eating his books. Before the trial he made a wick which he attached to the bag of deadly poison. When, at the conclusion of the trial, the verdict and sentence was announced he lit the wick and all those present in court inhaled the deadly vapour. This version of events is less plausible as it is unlikely that the prisoners and women and children would have been immune from the noxious poison.

21

Whatever the reason for the deaths, the court session of 6th July 1577 became known as the Black Assizes and all future Assizes were held at the Town Hall until the opening of the County Hall in 1841.

What of Rowland Jenkes? Well once he freed himself, minus ears, he travelled to London to work for a Catholic priest but once again was arrested and ended up in Oxford Gaol again.

On his release he travelled to Douai in Northern France then part of the Spanish Netherlands and a favourite destination for English Catholics after the accession of Elizabeth to the throne of England and the re-imposition of the Protestant faith.

The attraction was the English College, which was part of the University of Douai. Jenkes became the college baker until his death in 1610.

— 39 —

Oxford's Unrivalled Coffee Pedigree

1654

Oxford is full of Lewis Carroll-type absurdities such as the Tortoise Race at Corpus Christi College and The Mallard Ceremony at All Souls College.

So, it should be no surprise that two Oxford coffee houses opposite one another in Oxford's famous High Street ('The High') should make illogical claims about their longevity.

The Grand Café, next door to the Examination Schools, claims to be on the site of the oldest coffee house in England, having opened in 1651. Whilst the Queen's Lane Coffee House directly opposite the High and opened in 1654 claims to be the oldest coffee house in Europe.

One would have thought that if you were the oldest in Europe you would automatically be the oldest in England, so disqualifying The Grand Café's claim. However, the Queen's Lane Coffee House has operated continuously since 1654. So, by all normal rules is the oldest at every level.

What is now The Grand Café was opened in a room forming part of The Angel Inn, Oxford's principal coaching inn, by a Jew named Jacob. The Jews had at about that time been readmitted to England by Oliver Cromwell after an absence of 360 years, having been expelled by Edward I in 1290, for various trumped up charges to do with money lending.

Another Jew, named Jobson, opened a second coffee house, Queen's Lane Coffee House in 1654 which has traded continuously since then. The Grand Café on the other hand has since 1651 been an inn, a hotel, a grocer and most famously the Frank Cooper marmalade shop. Also it has been a Co-Op, a post office and the English Teddy Bear Shop. It wasn't until 1997 that it reverted to a coffee shop when The Grand Café opened.

It wasn't until the 17th century that the coffee bean was first brought to England by travellers returning from Arabia where its medicinal properties had long been recognised. It could cure or guard against smallpox, measles, headache, dropsy, gout and all manner of illnesses.

Coffee replaced beer as the drink to have with breakfast, water being unsafe to drink. Before the advent of coffee, a good proportion of the nation would no doubt have started the day drunk.

It has been suggested that Jacobs and Jobson were one of the same, but no clear proof exists. However, there is no doubt that Jacobs left Oxford in 1654 and opened a coffee house in London at the Old Southampton Buildings, Holborn, from where he was still trading in 1671.

By the end of the 17th century, thirteen coffee houses had opened in Oxford to be followed in the 18th century by another forty.

The main clientele of the coffee houses were the university students. The relaxed informal atmosphere was the major attraction, a welcome change from the monotony of university life.

The importance of the coffee house in gathering and distributing news and politics was reflected in the commercial success of the political newspapers that were largely dependent on the coffee houses, which made such publications freely available.

The colleges were soon urged by their students to provide similar facilities, thus influencing the creation of the college common room.

During the mid-18th century, the expansion of the trade with China and India led to the expansion of the tea trade, which was cheaper than coffee and precipitated the decline of the coffee house in favour of tea rooms selling food as well as tea.

However, since the late 20th century coffee has seen a great revival with the likes of Starbucks, Costa, Café Nero and Coffee Republic. But in Oxford, The Queen's Lane Coffee House and The Grand Café still lead the way with a pedigree that the newcomers cannot match.

— 40 —

The Dissenting Wesleys – Founders of Methodism

1727

Methodism was founded in Oxford in the late 1720s by two brothers, John Wesley (1703-1791) and Charles Wesley (1707-1788), later assisted by George Whitefield (1714-1770) one of their young disciples. John was a don at Lincoln College at the time having, like his brother, graduated from Christ Church where they were both ordained into the Anglican Church at Christ Church Cathedral. Whitfield was a graduate from Pembroke College.

John Wesley in 1727 returned home for two years to assist his father Samuel, who was Vicar of Epworth Parish in the Lincolnshire Fenlands, with the running of the parish.

In this time younger brother Charles formed a small group of Christians who met in each other's rooms to pray and study the Bible. When John returned to Oxford, he joined the group and became its leader. These were the seeds of Methodism.

The brothers came from a long line of Oxford educated Anglican dissenters or non-conformists, which can be traced back to their great grandfather Bartholomew (1596-1680) who graduated from Oxford where he had studied philosophy, physics and medicine. He was given the livings of Charmouth and Catherson by Cromwell's parliamentarians who he supported during the Civil War. However, he was totally non-conformist and refused to adopt the Book of Common Prayer, leading to his expulsion from Charmouth in 1665.

Bartholomew was the third son of Sir Herbert Wesley and Anne, the daughter of Sir Henry Colley, a close relation of the Primate of All Ireland. They had an only son, John (1636-1678) who studied at New Hall College, Oxford, where he graduated in 1657 when he was appointed an Evangelist. Like his father he gained the approval of Cromwell's Triers (Assessors of Parish Priests) and was appointed Vicar of Winterbourne in Dorset.

John Wesley was even more non-conformist than his father and was twice imprisoned for not using The Book of Prayer and, like his father, was ejected from Winterbourne Parish in 1665.

John married a relation of the Patriarch of Dorset and they had two sons. Their second son Samuel walked all the way to Oxford from Winterbourne and secured a job as a servitor (waiter) at Exeter College as a means of paying for his education there.

Samuel Wesley was ordained whilst at Exeter College and secured a living at Epworth in Lincolnshire. Amazingly he was even more rebellious than his father and grandfather. He preached sermons highly critical of the Church authorities for neglecting procedures and sacraments and their general laxness. He was a strict disciplinarian and insisted on a very principled code of personal conduct. He was also a first-rate poet and expressed his dissatisfaction through his poetry.

Samuel and his wife Suzanne had 19 children, ten of whom survived. Three of the survivors were sons Samuel, John and Charles. All attended Christ Church Oxford where they were ordained into the Anglican Church. It was John and Charles who made the big breakthrough and created the Methodist Church, which the actions of four generations of Wesleys had been leading to. It was like a small underground stream or aquifer looking for a point at which to spring forth into the open air.

John and Charles Wesley's gatherings were not just about Bible study and prayer; they were great adherents to 'The Great Commandment' of Jesus, "Though shalt love they neighbour". This manifested itself in visits to Oxford prisons, feeding and clothing poor people and fierce opposition to slavery.

The Wesley's group had to endure much ridicule from their fellow students who called them 'Bible Moths', 'The Holy Club', 'Sacramentarians' and 'Methodists'. This latter sobriquet meaning methodical, exceptionally detailed in their Bible study, opinions and disciplined lifestyle. They quite liked the Methodist description so happily adopted it as the name for their brand of Christianity.

Today Methodism is the fourth largest Christian denomination in Britain with 188,000 adherents. Worldwide there are 800 million followers, being particularly popular in the United States. In 1926, to commemorate the 200th anniversary of John Wesley's election to a fellowship at Lincoln College, Methodists in the United States paid for a 15th Century linen fold panelling to be installed in the room where he was thought to have given his tutorials.

They also had 18th century furniture installed. The room is situated in the south-east corner of the Front Quad and is vacated every afternoon so that visitors may see it. Unfortunately, recent historical evidence would suggest that he resided in another room in the Chapel Quad, but no matter, they got the right college and it is the symbolism that is important.

It is fitting that one of the most impressive (and most overlooked) buildings in Oxford is the Wesley Memorial Methodist Church, opened in 1878 and designed by Charles Bell. A fitting tribute to a family whose sheer persistence through four generations created one of the world's great Christian religions.

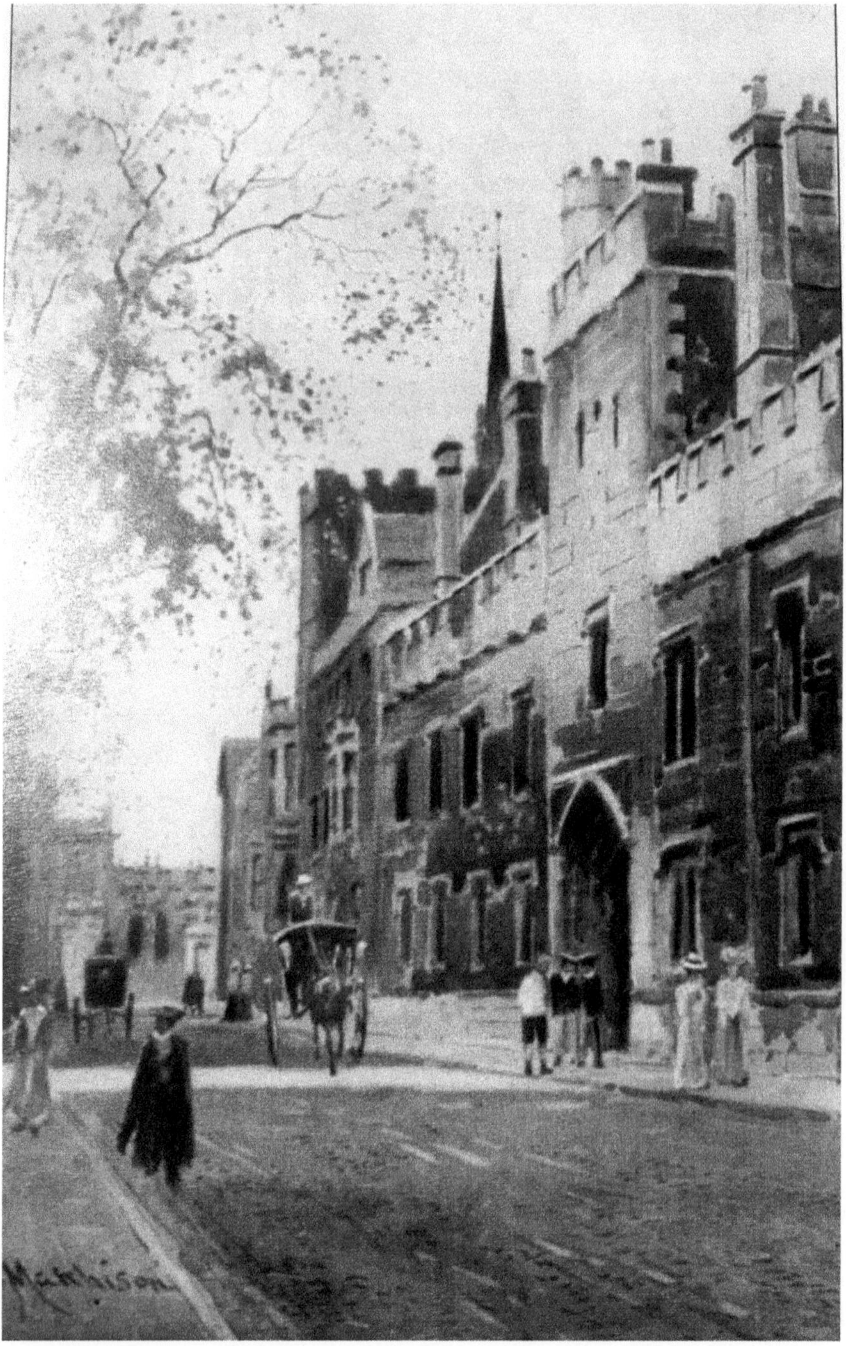

— 41 —

Deadmans Walk – Ghost Hunters' Delight

1645

If one wanted to create a ghost trail name, 'Deadman's Walk' would appear to have all the right ghoulish elements.

It is certainly spine-chilling, especially when uttered after dark. The subject is a dead man, a necessary prerequisite for any ghost, and a dedicated walkway is most useful when trying to locate the ghost.

Oxford of course has such a path named Deadman's Walk which runs between the surviving northern section of the Old City Wall in front of Merton College and Christ Church Meadow.

It used to be the route of the Jewish Funeral procession from the synagogue at St Aldates to the burial ground in what is now Magdalen's Botanic Gardens. Another useful element for ghost hunters is the Old City Wall which was the scene of many a battle and gruesome death.

Being outside the city wall it was considered a respectable place for Jews to be buried. Plenty of ghostly raw material there. Unfortunately, in 1290 Edward I banned the Jews from Oxford and the rest of England for allegedly coin clipping and extortion. They were not to return for another 400 years when Oliver Cromwell saw the commercial advantage of having the Jews back.

In the meantime, people were often executed along Deadman's Walk up against the Old City Wall. A most pleasing location with spectators able to picnic in Christ Church Meadow whilst they watched the entertainment.

The most famous ghost is Francis Windebank, a colonel in Charles I's Cavaliers who was executed by firing squad, by his own side, for surrendering to Cromwell's Roundheads. His ghost was quite regularly seen but he seems to have quietened down recently.

Another victim of the Civil War was a young puritan woman, Prudence Bostock, who is often sighted in Magpie Lane, which runs south from

Deadman's Walk between Merton and Corpus Christi Colleges to the High Street. She is believed to have died of a broken heart after her Cavalier lover ran away, and her ghost continues to roam Magpie Lane hoping for his return.

Also, from Deadman's Walk can sometimes be seen a light intermittently shining from Merton's Old Library, reputedly the oldest working library in the world, dating from 1371. This should not be possible because the library is locked after dark and nobody works in the library at night. This sanction goes back to the days of candlelight when candles were banned in the library in case the books were accidently burnt. It is thought that the light is being used by the ghost of Sir Thomas Bodley (1545-1613), a Fellow of Merton College and eventually in 1596 its Proctor. He became a distinguished diplomat, but he is chiefly remembered for the creation of the library that bears his name, the Bodleian, probably the most famous library in the world. Bodley is buried in Merton Chapel so he no doubt occasionally roams the library at night apologising for upstaging Merton's Old Library with his later and grander creation of 1602.

Another ghost who gallops up and down Deadman's Walk is George Napier. He was an alumnus of Corpus Christi and was hung, drawn and quartered in 1610 for being an active Roman Catholic. His head was impaled on either the spire of Christ Church or Tom Tower, nobody is quite sure. The reason for his frantic gallops up and down Deadman's Walk is a vain attempt to locate his head.

Deadman's Walk is definitely a rewarding area for ghost hunters.

g# — 42 —

Mary Blandy – Don't Hang Me High

1752

On Monday 6th April 1752 Mary Blandy, aged 31, was hung for the murders of her father Francis Blandy, the Town Clerk of Henley and eminent lawyer. He was poisoned.

This was a very unusual case in as much as such crimes were usually committed by the lower classes, not members of the establishment.

What drove this sophisticated and well-educated young woman to murder her own father? The answer is love; a love forbidden by her father.

The object of Mary's love was a penniless captain, William Henry Cranstoun, the younger son of Lord Cranstoun and his wife Lady Jane Ker. They had first met in 1746 when Captain Cranstoun was visiting his uncle, Sir Mark Ker, in his Henley residence Paradise House. At the time he showed no particular interest in his uncle's attractive neighbour.

What changed his attitude was Mary's father deciding it was high time his daughter was married before she was left on the shelf. So, he embarked on a marketing exercise which involved him in making out he was even wealthier than he already was by advertising a dowry of £10,000; a huge sum for those days, for the man who married Mary, thus making his daughter an extremely desirable marriage prospect. In the 18th century wealthy families, to secure their estates, very much married for money. Francis Blandy was seeking a wealthy young aristocrat for his daughter.

It certainly did the trick as far as Captain Cranstoun was concerned. He began courting Mary in earnest and she in turn fell helplessly in love with him. However, he wasn't quite what her father had in mind. For a start he looked years older than 38 due to a disfigurement of his facial features caused by smallpox. And more important, although he was aristocratic, he had no money.

Nevertheless, he had a certain charm and a way with words which greatly appealed to Mary. Her mother quite liked him as well. It is said that women fall in love with their ears and men with their eyes. So, despite father's disapproval, Mary was adamant she wanted to marry Captain Cranstoun.

Then came the final straw as far as Mary's father was concerned, when it turned out that he had a wife and child in Scotland and also an illegitimate child in London. Cranstoun was told never to darken the Blandy doorstep again and Mary was strictly forbidden to ever see him again.

It turned out that Cranstoun had married in 1745 and as a result of his serious interest in Mary had the marriage annulled in 1748 on payment of alimony of 40 shillings a week.

None of this dampened Mary's ardour for Cranstoun who had returned to Scotland to finalise his divorce.

It is at this point that matters became contentious as the lovers devised a plan to remove the obstacle of Mary's father's disapproval. According to Mary, Cranstoun sent her a quantity of white powder which he said was a love potion and that she was to stir it into his food. This Cranstoun assured her would induce a spirit of goodwill and bonhomie in her father such that he would give their wedding plans his blessing.

In reality the white powder was arsenic and within days of consuming it with his food, he died on 14th August 1751. Mary's mother had died earlier in the year of a fever so was unaffected. Unfortunately for Mary, two of the servants had observed her tampering with her father's food and when the post-mortem was carried out, arsenic was discovered in the dead man's stomach. As the two servants had eaten some of the food and became ill, Mary was arrested and taken to Oxford Castle.

Mary was held in the castle until the next Assizes which was not until 3rd March 1752. However, because of her social standing she was afforded her own room and allowed to have one of her maids with her to see to her needs. She was even allowed to have visitors for afternoon tea.

She came to trial before the Honourable Hornage Legg Esq and Sir Sidney Stafford Smith. The trial was of particular interest because it was the first time medical evidence had been presented in court in a case of murder by poisoning.

Mary defended herself with the help of three counsel with what had been described as intelligence and zeal although her case was hopeless, particularly as the servants had seen her trying to destroy the evidence, which one of them had recovered and which was used in evidence.

At the end of a one day 13-hour trial the jury convicted her of murder and hanged in the Castle Yard on 6th April 1752. Her last request to the officials was "for the sake of decency gentleman don't hang me high". She was concerned that the men in the crowd would look up her skirts if she was too high. She apparently behaved with great bravery and penitence to the end and protested her innocence to the crowd before she was turned off.

By a strange irony Captain Cranstoun died not long after Mary. He had fled to Flanders where, sheltering in a convent, he died of a mysterious illness which caused his limbs to swell up and drove him out of his mind.

It still remains a matter of conjecture as to which of the two lovers was the true culprit. Mary was an intelligent and knowledgeable woman who surely would not have been so easily tricked by Cranstoun or was Cranstoun the one who was duped by a determined woman or was it truly a lover's pact? We will never know.

— 43 —

Woodstock – Sporting Royal Palace

849AD

Woodstock, a town 10 miles north of Oxford, has always been closely associated with the city, particularly since Norman times. The reason for this close association is the presence of a Hunting Lodge, much used by royalty for over 700 years.

The Hunting Lodge predates the Normans, for it is recorded that the later Saxon kings were frequent visitors. King Alfred 'the Great' (849-899) was a regular visitor, and it is recorded that he translated the Roman philosopher Boethius' *The Consolation of Philosophy* in 888AD whilst staying at Woodstock.

Henry I (the Conqueror's fourth son) built Beaumont Palace in Oxford in 1131 to provide comfortable accommodation whilst the royals and their friends were visiting the nearby Woodstock Hunting Lodge, which at that time was a little primitive, although its location (situated in the picturesque Glyme Valley) was very pleasing.

Henry I built an enormous seven-mile wall to create Britain's first enclosed park, to keep the animals in and the people out. The people who had lived in the park were summarily evicted. With the greater security, Henry was able to introduce more exotic animals such as leopards, lions and porcupines.

It was Queen Matilda's son, Henry II (1133-1189), however, who decided to convert the Woodstock Hunting Lodge into a Royal Palace, spending a colossal £4,000 on its construction. This even exceeded what he had spent on his brand new palace at Greenwich. Why spend so much on a palace so far from London? The answer was that Henry was a keen huntsman and falconer, and the huge herds of deer present must have been a great attraction. The geographically central position in England and the distance from plague-ridden towns were other attractions. Also, it made the perfect lovers' retreat for Henry and The Fair Rosamund, the love of Henry's life.

All of the Plantagenet kings, from Henry II in 1154 to Richard III in 1485, were regular visitors to Woodstock, and the Tudors, when they came to power, were also frequent visitors.

In 1494, Henry VII, the first Tudor king, was at Woodstock planning the three-year old future Henry VIII's investiture as the Duke of York. This was to counter claims by the pretender Perkin Warbeck that he, as the surviving, younger prince in the Tower, was the true Duke of York. And then, in 1497, on a truly auspicious occasion, Prince Arthur (the heir to the throne) was formally betrothed to the Spanish Catherine of Aragon. The choice of Woodstock for this great event, of much international importance, would indicate that this was no mere hunting lodge but one of the most spectacular residences in the land.

It is almost certainly the case that Henry VIII, in a final attempt to seduce Anne Boleyn, took her to Woodstock in July 1531 for a prolonged stay. It is thought probable that Anne was pregnant when she and Henry went through a nuptial ceremony in January 1533. Henry VIII continued to be a regular visitor until later in his reign, when increasing immobility (caused by his painful legs and obesity) restricted his journeys to manor houses nearest to London.

Woodstock deteriorated through neglect during the reigns of Henry VIII's children, Edward VI and Mary I. It was next used as a place of confinement for Princess Elizabeth, who had originally been imprisoned in the Tower of London by her sister, the Catholic Mary I. Elizabeth was detained at Woodstock from May 1554 until April 1555, guarded by 100 soldiers.

It was Mary's Spanish husband, Philip, who persuaded her to release Elizabeth, fearing Mary, Queen of Scots, an enemy of Spain, more than Elizabeth. In any case, Mary I died within a year of Elizabeth's release.

Elizabeth rarely visited during her reign and Woodstock deteriorated further. Elizabeth's successor, James I, enjoyed his sport and stayed at Woodstock in most years of his reign, but just renovated a few rooms for himself in the ruinous mansion, leaving his court to sleep under canvas.

Charles I became a regular visitor during the war with Cromwell's parliamentarians. For the duration of the Civil War Oxford was Charles I's seat of government and the royal garrison, with Woodstock as a second line of defence.

The Civil War was the undoing of Woodstock. It suffered war damage and the victorious Cromwell allowed it to crumble. Much looting took place during the Puritans' regime and hunting lost its popularity.

Fifty years later in 1704, the Woodstock estate was transformed as a result of the 'Battle of Blenheim', won by a victorious John Churchill. Queen Anne made him Duke of Marlborough and gave him the Manor of Woodstock, including the ruins of the old palace. A grateful parliament provided the money to build a new palace on a site some distance away from the ruins of the old one.

Designed by Sir John Vanburgh in the English Baroque style, it is one of the largest houses in England with a park and gardens to match. It has been the home of the Churchill family for the last 300 years and is notable as the birthplace of Sir Winston Churchill.

Every trace of Woodstock Palace was removed in 1720, not a brick or a stone remains. In 1961 a stone plinth was put up to mark the site of the old palace where England's kings and queens for over 700 years took their leisure. No other palace can match it for longevity except Greenwich.

— 44 —

St Giles' Fair – The Biggest Fair in England

1624

St Giles' Fair is a throwback to mediaeval England's great country fairs. It evolved in the second half of the 18th century from the St Giles' Parish Wake, which is first recorded in 1624. In the 1780s it was a toy fair and by the 19th century had become a general fair for children.

By the 1830s, however, it began to cater more for adults with the introduction of entertainment (a forerunner of the later music halls). It also provided opportunities to buy clothing, crockery, tools and even sewing machines.

It is held on the first Monday and Tuesday of September unless it falls on the Feast of St Giles, then it is moved to the following Monday and Tuesday.

If your name is Giles and the four digits of the year add up to the age of the reigning monarch, then you can ask for a free ride.

In the 17th and 18th centuries these fairs were often hiring fairs where you could hire farmworkers such as draymen or farriers, who would carry a tool of their trade. Thomas Hardy's *Jude the Obscure* illustrates this aspect of the fair.

The great fairs were held in the autumn, when the harvest was over and the poor had some money to spend on the ubiquitous sideshows.

Governments cannot interfere with these ancient fairs without a special Act of Parliament and when a Home Secretary tried to cancel the fair in 1914, he was told he had no such power so the fair went ahead.

The present fair is organised by Oxford City Council and the London and Home Counties' Section of the Showmen's Guild of Great Britain.

St Giles' pedigree is, in fact, older than the officially recorded dates of 1624 and 1830 mentioned earlier. The origins of the fair related to St Giles' Church which was consecrated in 1200. As part of the consecration St Giles' Fair was established. In fact, Queen Elizabeth I stayed in Oxford between 3rd-10th September 1567 and watched the fair from the windows of St John's College on the east side of St Giles.

From the 1830s, with the inclusion of adult amusements such as song and dance acts and terpsichorean artistes, this was, in a sense, a forerunner of the music hall. They became rowdy and were not popular with everybody, and vain attempts were made to have them banned.

John Betjeman, writing in 1937, observed that, "It is the biggest fair in England. The whole of St Giles and even Magdalen Street right up to the War Memorial at the meeting of Woodstock and Banbury Roads, is thick with freak shows, roundabouts, cake walks, the whip and witching waves. Every sort of fairman finds it worth his while to come to St Giles."

Today the freak shows no longer exist, but as well as traditional rides such as the big wheel, dodgems, helter-skelter and carousel, there are the state-of-the-art white-knuckle rides.

For two days all the roads hosting the fair are closed to vehicular traffic, and miraculously everything returns to normal in time for the rush hour on the third day.

— 45 —

The First English Civil War

1142

Oxford Castle was built in 1071 by one of William the Conqueror's loyal lieutenants, Robert D'Oilly, in the thriving market town of Oxford.

William had recognised the strategic importance of Oxford, which was situated downstream to the west of London in the centre of England, and in the pathway of armies on their way to London. It was, therefore, important to ensure that Oxford was properly defended with a Norman motte-and-bailey castle.

D'Oilly chose as the site the West Gate of the existing town wall with its imposing St George's Tower already in situ, which he incorporated into the castle design. D'Oilly also built St George's Church within the curtilage of the castle on the site of an Anglo-Saxon church. Only the crypt with its Romanesque arches remains.

St George's Tower, until recently, was thought to have been built contemporaneously with the castle, but it was observed recently to have been archaeologically at odds with the rest of the castle's buildings and other Norman towers in England. The Anglo-Saxon St George's Tower is probably the oldest secular structure in England.

However, it is an escape of the most ingenious nature from St George's Tower, made by Empress Matilda in 1142, that is of particular interest. It was at the height of the Civil War with her cousin Stephen over the succession to the English throne after the death of Henry I in 1135, that Matilda's feat of derring-do was accomplished.

The Civil War, known as The Anarchy, lasted for twenty years between Matilda (daughter of Henry I) and Stephen (son of Adela, Henry I's sister); both were grandchildren of the Conqueror.

The problem was Salic Law, which was developed in France and excluded all females from the succession. Although the Normans as Vikings did not necessarily subscribe to it, they did not take kindly to women's rule, hence Stephen's claim to the English throne.

Unknown Oxford

The battle between Empress Matilda and King Stephen (who had been crowned on 22nd December 1135) raged backwards and forwards for twenty years, with Matilda capturing Stephen in 1129 and then releasing him in exchange for her half-brother Robert, who had been captured by Stephen's forces.

Empress Matilda (or Maud, as the English styled her) was never crowned, because the citizens of London refused her entry into the capital. Her title of Empress came as a result of her marriage at the age of thirteen to Henry IV, the Holy Roman Emperor and King of Germany. On his death ten years later, Matilda married Geoffrey of Anjou in order to consolidate her father's power in Normandy, but the union was not popular with the English barons.

In many ways, Empress Matilda had the perfect credentials for an English monarch because her mother (Henry I's first wife) was the daughter of Malcolm II of Scotland – a member of the West Saxon Royal Family and a descendant of Alfred the Great. So with both Norman and Anglo-Saxon genes, she would have seemed to be ideal to be Queen of an Anglo/Norman kingdom, except she was a woman and, therefore, beyond the pale.

However, Matilda and Geoffrey had a son, Henry, who distinguished himself on the battlefield fighting his mother's cause. He was to prove to be the key to the eventual settlement of the Civil War.

Having set the scene we return to Oxford Castle in 1142, where Empress Matilda had sought refuge as the guest of one of her supporters, Robert D'Oilly, the nephew of the now-deceased Robert D'Oilly who had built the castle.

It was not long before Stephen had tracked Matilda down and surrounded the castle in a siege that lasted for three months, designed to starve her into submission. But Stephen had not reckoned with Matilda's next move, a daring and most cunning escape. It was midwinter and the snow lay thick on the ground. So, in white gowns, she and several trusted knights were lowered by rope from the top of St George's Tower onto a frozen River Thames and on to Abingdon and safety.

They were not detected by Stephen's surrounding forces because of their white garments, which merged into the snowy landscape.

This escape ensured that the war continued with Matilda's claim intact. It also proved fundamental to the future of both English and European history.

The war raged on for another eleven years before Matilda's son Henry, now married to Eleanor of Aquitaine, in 1153 came across to England and surprised Stephen with an ingenious offer: Stephen could remain King until his death, provided he adopted Henry as his son and heir. Stephen's own son, Eustace, had died five months earlier, so the only possible obstacle had been removed. Stephen's agreement to this plan was encapsulated in the Treaty of Westminster.

Stephen died on 25th October 1154, when Henry succeeded to the Crown with no difficulty or competing claims.

Henry II was crowned in 1154 and with the Royal blood of the Conqueror and Alfred the Great in his veins, he was to become one of England's greatest kings.

— 46 —

Oxford – Colin Dexter's Crime Capital of Europe

1975

At 8pm on 6th January 1987, Colin Dexter, an examiner with the Oxford Examining Board, who wrote crime novels in his spare time, suddenly hit the big time.

On that fateful night Central Television launched a detective series like no other, entitled *Morse*, adapted from the novels of Colin Dexter and featuring Chief Inspector Morse.

This first episode, entitled *The Dead of Jericho*, was the fifth of the seven Morse novels Dexter had written at that time. He was to write a total of thirteen Morse novels before he killed off his hero in 1999.

The television series was to spawn a total of thirty-three episodes, twelve based on Dexter's novels. Dexter supplied the plot lines for seven other episodes.

At its peak Morse attracted 750 million viewers worldwide in forty-six countries.

Of great significance was the physical presence of Oxford with its magnificent and varied architecture, 'the city of dreaming spires' as Matthew Arnold described it in his poem *Thyrsis*. It was a film maker's dream – so photogenic.

The two main characters were played by two actors already known to the public: John Thaw (playing the eponymous Chief Inspector Morse) and Kevin Whately (playing his sidekick Sergeant Robbie Lewis).

Thaw had gained fame in the 1970s as Inspector Jack Regan of the Flying Squad in a series entitled *The Sweeney*. It was characterised by endless car chases, punch-ups and seedy East London pubs. Whately had played a Geordie, which he was, in a comedy series entitled *Auf Wiedersehen Pet*, which appeared on Central Television in the mid-1980s.

The only thing that Morse and Jack Regan had in common was their excessive alcohol intake. Colin Dexter's Morse was a totally different kettle of fish: crosswords, Wagner and literature of the 19th century, particularly AE Housman and Thomas Hardy, were his favourite writers; Morse was addicted to real ale (London Pride was his favourite), malt whisky and the radio series *The Archers*. All first novels tend to be semi-autobiographical and this was certainly the case with Morse, some of whose characteristics were those of his creator Colin Dexter.

After the end of Morse a sequel emerged based on a Dexter short story. *Lewis*, Morse's long-suffering sidekick, was promoted to Inspector and this spawned 33 episodes with Lewis given a sidekick of his own, Sgt Hathaway, played by Laurence Fox (of the Fox dynasty: Edward, James and Emelia). This ran from 2006 to 2015 and then, seamlessly, a prequel was born, *Endeavour*, the story of young Morse's early days in the Oxford Police Force set in the sixties. Endeavour has so far produced 26 episodes and stars Shaun Evans playing the young Morse; Endeavour was Morse's Christian name, which he never used.

But what of the genesis for all this television success, Colin Dexter, from where did he emerge?

Colin Dexter was born on 29th September 1930 in Stamford, Lincolnshire. His father ran a small garage and taxi business. He had an elder brother, John, who taught Classics at King's School, Peterborough, and a sister, Avril. He gained a scholarship to Stamford School, a minor public school, where he excelled academically and also played rugby for the school's first fifteen.

On leaving school Dexter completed his National Service with the Royal Signal Corps, becoming a high speed Morse code operator in Germany. He then completed his education at Christ's College, Cambridge, where he read Classics, earning a Bachelor's degree in 1953 and a Master's in 1958, whilst teaching Classics at Wyggeston School in Leicester.

In 1956 he married Dorothy Cooper, by whom he had a daughter, Sally, and a son, Jeremy. And then in 1966 when he was senior Classics teacher at Corby Grammar School, his teaching career was cut short by incipient deafness. This was to prove to be one of life's watershed moments, resulting in him coming to Oxford to take up a post with the Oxford Examining Board where he remained for the next 22 years. During this time he became a part-time writer of crime novels.

He started by writing a few pages of what was to turn out to be his first Morse novel, *Last Bus to Woodstock*, whilst on holiday in Wales when a week of continuous rainfall enabled him to read two crime novels. He concluded that they were not very good and that he could do better. The year was 1972 and it was to be another two years before he finished this seminal work. He found a publisher, MacMillan, at the second attempt; Collins turned *Woodstock* down.

Last Bus to Woodstock received favourable reviews and he wrote six more novels before Central Television came knocking on the door, in the shape of Kenny McBain. He was intrigued by the central character, Chief Inspector Morse, whose name came about as a result of Dexter's love of crosswords: from 1965 to 1975 Dexter and Sir Jeremy Morse, chairman of Lloyds Bank, alternated as national crossword champions. Dexter also set the Observer crossword for many years. Incidentally, a Mrs B Lewis was also a noted crossword compiler at this time. The book's two main characters were Morse and Lewis!

The third main character was the City of Oxford, but Central Television made some crucial additions and changes which were to be of great significance.

Throughout each episode classical music was to be in the background and a haunting theme tune was to be a key constituent, with its Morse code repetition at the beginning and end. The composer was a young Australian, Barrington Pheloung, who has written the incidental music to all of the *Morse*, *Lewis* and *Endeavour* television plays.

Morse's Lancia was swapped for a maroon Jaguar 2.4, and Lewis, instead of being a contemporary of Morse in age, became a much younger man, leading to a generational gap, creating a sort of father/son relationship.

Dexter was not consulted on these changes but he did not object, he was just glad to see his name up in lights and his books adapted for the small screen. and he thought the casting of John Thaw was one of the keys to the success of the Morse TV series, particularly the emphasis on the middle-aged bachelor who needed looking after by the 'Right Woman'. He fell in love with practically every attractive woman he met, to no avail; he could commit but not compromise.

He had been badly hurt when jilted in his student days at St John's College, Oxford, so much so that he never sat his final examinations.

He remained a dysfunctional bachelor living in his North Oxford house and living on a diet of alcohol and takeaways. Many women amongst the television viewers wanted to mother him.

In the books and television series there is an intriguing connection between Colin Dexter's alma mater, Stamford School, and the fictional Lonsdale College. The latter featured in seven episodes, and from the author's precise geographical references, Brasenose College is obviously the model. The original, famous brazen nose sanctuary knocker, from which Brasenose derives its name, was taken to Stamford in 1334 by the Master and scholars, who were themselves seeking sanctuary from the continual rioting between town and gown which characterised Oxford in the 13th and 14th centuries. Edward II did not approve of the setting-up of a rival seat of learning in Stamford so forced the dissident scholars back to Oxford, but the knocker was overlooked and did not return to Oxford until 1890. In the meantime it became part of Stamford School, being affixed to Stamford House which was put up for auction in 1890 and bought by Brasenose College just to get the knocker back. It now holds pride of place above High Table. A replica was made and resides in Stamford in place of the original, a tale Dexter would have been aware of when a pupil at Stamford, hence Lonsdale/Brasenose College.

All of Dexter's books were made into television plays, except *The Secret of Annexe 3*. Central Television hesitated a long while before making *The Wench is Dead* because of the expense involved. It concerns the solving of a fictional Oxford canal murder of 1840, by Morse when in hospital with a burst ulcer. Dexter readily acknowledges that his inspiration was the Josephine Tey novel *The Daughter of Time*, written in 1951 in which her hero, Inspector Grant, laid up in bed with broken bones, passed his time by proving that Richard III did not murder The Princes in the Tower. It was voted by The Crime Writers' Association the best crime novel of all time. Dexter received a Gold Dagger from the same body for *The Wench is Dead* so the pressure to make the more expensive story, with its switching from 1840 to the present, became irresistible. It was the only episode in which Kevin Whately did not appear.

The other intriguing feature was that Colin Dexter appeared, Hitchcock style, in every episode somewhere in the background.

One book, *The Jewel that was Ours*, was inspired by the television episode entitled *The Wolvercote Tongue* written by Julian Mitchell. Dexter's book first appeared in 1991, three years after Julian Mitchell's television play had been screened. It also had a different ending. Julian Mitchell wrote the screenplays for ten episodes of Morse. He was also an Oxford Alumnus having graduated from Wadham College.

In fact, the screenwriters for the Morse series reads like a Who's Who of British screenwriters: Anthony Minghella (*The English Patient*), Danny Boyle (*Trainspotting*), Malcolm Bradbury (*The History Man*) and Alma Cullen (*A Village Affair*).

After the conclusion of the Morse TV series in 2000, in which Morse dies of a heart attack, the actor who played him, John Thaw, died from oesophageal cancer in 2002.

It was Colin Dexter who suggested the sequel *Lewis* and was a special adviser on the prequel *Endeavour*. He appeared in many of the episodes in his customary cameo role, until his death on 21st March 2017 at the age of 86.

Of his 13 Morse novels, two received Silver Daggers from The Crime Writers' Association, two were awarded Gold Daggers and he also received a Cartier Diamond Dagger for lifetime achievement.

In 2000, Dexter received the OBE for services to literature, and in 2001 he was awarded the Freedom of the City of Oxford, quite an achievement for a Cambridge man.

— 47 —

Oxford – Royal Capital of England

1642-1646

King Charles I was much influenced by a pamphlet that his father, King James I, had written entitled 'The Trew Law of Monarchies', which concluded "that the king was above the law". His father never put it into practice, but his son did, dissolving Parliament in 1625 having decided that he could do quite well without its interference.

He couldn't, because he needed money to conduct a war with Scotland, so Parliament was recalled in 1640 (The Long Parliament), but it would not grant him the money to fund his war with Scotland. This was the catalyst for the English Civil War.

In early January 1642 Charles left London to seek a safer base from which to conduct his war with the Parliamentarians. He vainly tried to capture London at the Battle of Edgehill which ended in a stalemate. The Royalists withdrew to Oxford.

Charles entered Oxford on 29th October 1642 and it was his military headquarters and seat of government for the next four years. He personally took up residence at Christ Church and held court there, and this is where the newly-formed Parliament met.

Many of the Oxford colleges were used for specific purposes; Oriel was where the Privy Council met. The Law and Logic Schools became granaries, and New College was used as a powder magazine. Magdalen College grove became an artillery park and All Souls an arsenal. Brasenose became a food store. Jesus College provided accommodation for people of quality from Wales. St John's College played host to Prince Rupert.

The university broadly supported the Royalist cause while the townsfolk were largely supporters of the Parliamentarians.

It cost the university dear because Charles needed money to finance the war. Having coughed-up close on £2,000 initially, it was to be followed by a subvention of £1,176 a week from University Colleges. A Royal Mint was established at New Inn Hall Street and the colleges had to give up their gold and silver plate, which was melted down and transformed into the new Oxford Coinage. In all, plate weighing 2,000lb was melted down. One college, Corpus Christi, managed to hide its plate and now possesses the only collection of Renaissance silver in Oxford.

By 1645 most of the scholars had returned home, and Oxford effectively ceased to be a place of learning.

Queen Henrietta Maria arrived in Oxford in July 1643 with money, supplies, ammunition and 200 men from the north, and took up residence in Merton College, where a hole in the wall was made so she could visit her husband next door in Christ Church.

Oxford Castle was used for holding Parliamentarian prisoners of war. It soon attracted a reputation for its brutality and appalling conditions; prisoners were forced to answer the call of nature where they stood. Bodies of dead prisoners were left decomposing among the living.

On 7th May 1645 Charles set out from Oxford with a large part of his army to fight the decisive Battle of Naseby, in which he lost, losing the bulk of his army, 1,000 killed and 5,000 captured out of a total of 7,400. He returned to Oxford, which was then under siege by Sir Thomas Fairfax and Oliver Cromwell. Charles I escaped in April 1646 but was captured by the Scottish Presbyterian army at Newark, who eventually handed him over to the Parliamentarians in January 1647, in exchange for £100,000.

The remaining Royalists in Oxford, including Prince Rupert, finally surrendered on 20th June 1646. This ended Oxford's distinction of being the twin capital of England with London for four years, leaving the city and university substantially poorer, and the monarch (Charles I) some years later without a head.

— 48 —

Amy Robsart's Mysterious Death and the Virgin Queen's Favourite Courtier

1560

On the floor of the Chancel of St Mary the Virgin Church in Oxford (the University Church), there is a small marble tile, easily missed, bearing the inscription:

> "In a vault of brick at the upper end of this Quire was buried Amy Robsart wife of Lord Robert Dudley KG on Sunday 22 September 1560 AD"

This is all that remains of Amy's tomb which was, over time, dismantled and forgotten.

What has not been forgotten, however, are the circumstances of her death, one of the greatest mysteries of late mediaeval England. Accident, suicide, or murder?

What has made it so intriguing are the participants in this contentious possible homicide: the Queen of England, Queen Elizabeth I, and Amy's husband, the royal favourite Robert Dudley, the Earl of Leicester.

On 8th September 1560 Amy Dudley, née Robsart, whilst staying at Cumnor Place, three miles west of Oxford, fell down a flight of eight stairs and sustained a broken neck, from which she died.

Her death, under normal circumstances, would have been extremely convenient for Elizabeth and Robert Dudley's purposes, a marriage between two people who were deeply in love.

It must be remembered that in 1560 Elizabeth had only been on the throne for two years and was more receptive to the prospect of sharing power with a husband, particularly one whom she has known so well and loved.

However, because of the circumstances of Amy's death, marriage to Robert Dudley was impossible. It wasn't how it was supposed to happen.

Although only 28, the same age as Elizabeth and Dudley, Amy was suffering from breast cancer and was not expected to live for very long. So a marriage between Elizabeth and Robert, after a decent period of mourning, would have been perfectly acceptable.

Dudley, as the Queen's Master of Horse, was constantly in her company and he hardly saw his wife. Elizabeth was extremely demanding and would not let Dudley out of her sight. He was her closest unofficial advisor at Court – much to Chancellor Lord Cecil's chagrin. So it was obvious where things were heading.

And yet, ten years earlier, it had been so different when Amy and Robert had married. Two 18-year olds deeply in love, their wedding ceremony graced by the presence of Robert's childhood companion and classmate, Edward VI. It was a marriage made in heaven.

Robert's father was John, Duke of Northumberland, the most powerful man in the land as de facto Regent for the 13-year old Edward VI. Amy's father, Sir John Robsart, was a wealthy gentleman farmer in Norfolk where he owned vast estates.

A match made in heaven, and so it was until 1553 when the young couple's world was turned upside down with the death of Edward VI. The Duke of

Northumberland immediately installed Lady Jane Grey as Queen, after first marrying the unfortunate girl to his second youngest son, Guildford. It was not a popular move with the people.

Jane's reign lasted only a matter of days before Edward VI's elder sister Mary seized the throne and The Duke of Northumberland and his five sons were arrested. All were sentenced to death for treason.

The Duke of Northumberland, Lady Jane Grey and her husband were executed. Robert Dudley remained in the Tower of London for 18 months under sentence of death. Amy was, however, allowed to visit her husband, although the couple were now penniless, Robert having been attaindered, losing all property and hereditary titles. Fortunately, Amy's parents came to the rescue so she had a home to go to and financial support.

As might be expected, the Catholic Queen Mary's sister, the Protestant Elizabeth, was sent to the Tower for three months because she posed a potential threat. Mary's new husband, Philip II of Spain, persuaded her to release Elizabeth from the Tower and to be placed under house arrest at Woodstock. Five months later Robert Dudley was released and fought Philip II's Spanish cause in France, thus ingratiating himself with the new royal regime.

It is quite possible that Robert Dudley and Elizabeth met whilst both were imprisoned in the Tower. Within five years Queen Mary died. So, in 1558, Elizabeth became Queen and appointed Robert Dudley her Master of Horse; was this the beginning of the end for Amy Dudley?

For centuries the exact cause of Amy's death has been debated by historians, with the majority favouring the Coroner Court's jury verdict of accidental death. That is, until 2008 when the historian Chris Skidmore discovered the coroner's report in the National Archives at Kew. It revealed that Amy had sustained two wounds to the head, one half-a-thumb deep and the other two-thumbs deep. These injuries had not been mentioned in the original coroner's jury findings.

It had taken them a year to reach their verdict of accidental death; clearly the exact circumstances of her death were a matter of serious conjecture, particularly with two serious head wounds.

Despite the inquest's outcome Robert Dudley was, at the time, widely suspected of having organised his wife's death, but most modern historians support the findings of the inquest – accidental death.

The 2008 evidence in the form of the discovery of the coroner's report, is consistent with all three possible scenarios: accidental death, suicide or murder, so is of no great help.

Finally, the scene of Amy Dudley's death, Cumnor Place, was allegedly haunted by her ghost, so much so that nine Oxfordshire parsons came to Cumnor to exorcise her ghost, laying it to rest in a nearby pond, which has never since frozen over, even in the most severe winters.

Despite the exorcism Cumnor Place had a most uncongenial atmosphere, so much so that it became uninhabitable and was allowed to fall into disrepair until it was demolished in 1810. Some of its remains were used to rebuild the nearby Wytham Church, particularly the 14th century east window.

Amy Dudley's death is still one of the great mediaeval mysteries but whatever the true cause Elizabeth and Robert Dudley never did marry, but remained close until Dudley's death in 1588. This despite Dudley marrying the Queen's cousin Laetitia Knollys, the widow of the first Earl of Essex in 1578, when it was clear that Elizabeth had no intention of marrying.

— 49 —

Britain's Greatest Industrialist and Most Generous Philanthropist

1937

Lord Nuffield, born William Richard Morris, from humble beginnings as a bicycle repairer in his parents' house in Headington, was to become Britain's greatest industrialist ever.

He also became Britain's most generous philanthropist, on a scale only matched at the time by Andrew Carnegie and Nelson Rockefeller. In fact Nuffield's benefactions amounted to the equivalent of over £2 bn in today's money (2019).

He was born in Worcester in 1877, the eldest of seven children born to Frederick and Emily Morris. The family moved back to Oxford in 1880 where William was educated at the local Headington School. The family were working class; Frederick was a clerk, and although not poor certainly couldn't afford to satisfy William's desire to study medicine. So he became apprenticed to an Oxford bicycle dealer and repairer. After only one year he left, over a row about a pay increase, and set up on his own from a shed in his parents' garden.

In the next 20 years this expanded in the centre of Oxford to building and repairing bicycles and then motor bikes, and finally motor cars. He was a skilled mechanic, but above all he was a successful entrepreneur.

In the beginning, in order to promote his bicycles, he took to racing on his own hand-made bikes, competing as far away as south London. At one point he was Champion of Oxford (city and county), Berkshire and Buckinghamshire.

By 1902 he had showroom premises at 48 The High Street, and a garage on Longwall Street, built for him by the landlord, Merton College. It was here he designed his first Morris Oxford car. He sold 400 from blueprints at the 1912 Motor Show in London, and in order to build them he was able to borrow £4,000 from the Earl of Macclesfield, who as an Oxford undergraduate had hired a car from Morris in 1905. WRM Motors produced 1,300 cars in 1913 and quickly outgrew the Longwall premises, so in 1906 he rented a former army college in Cowley as the site for a new factory.

He decided from the beginning to outsource all components, mainly from the Midlands, and then assembling the Morris Oxford cars so that by 1914 he was showing healthy profits.

Between 1914 and 1918 he mass-produced munitions, receiving an OBE in 1917.

After the war his success came quickly as a result of two key moves. He adopted the mass-production techniques of Henry Ford in America and slashed the sale price of his cars by 30%, a huge risk at the time. He also concentrated on cars with smaller engines, which the UK tax system favoured. In 1920 Henry Ford had two-thirds of the UK car market, but Morris's bold initiatives paid off, so much so that by 1924 he overtook Ford to become the UK's biggest car manufacturer with a 51% share of the UK market.

In 1928 he was selling 55,000 cars annually. His nearest British competitor, Austin, was producing only a third of that, and Singer less than half of Austin's. By 1930 he employed over 10,000 people, and his Cowley works was transforming Oxford from a quiet university town to a substantial modern city. During the 1920s he had taken over more of his suppliers and competitors, most notably Wolseley.

His empire was outgrowing his brand of management, 'enlightened dictatorship'. He now had an army of middle managers, principally Leonard Lord whom he had recruited in 1923 and who was, unlike Morris, a 'modern management man'.

In 1934 Morris was raised to the peerage as Baron Nuffield, a name chosen by him from the hamlet of Nuffield, to where he had moved in 1933 to a manor house he renamed Nuffield Place.

He had gone public in 1926 but kept the majority of shares himself. In 1936 he moved to a big public flotation when everything became the Nuffield Organisation, with Nuffield himself still the biggest single shareholder and chairman. Leonard Lord was Managing Director. However, the two fell out and Lord went to Austin where he transformed the company, almost on a par with Morris. The two companies were to merge in 1952 to become the British Motor Corporation.

In 1939 the Nuffield Organisation was still ahead of the game but Nuffield himself had developed his philanthropic interests and his great days in the industry were over.

Nuffield's personal life was not a happy one. He had married Elizabeth Ansley in 1904; they had no children and she was a shy retiring woman who took pleasure in gardening and looking after their dogs. She was rarely seen with him in public and they gradually grew apart.

He made a sea voyage every winter to Australia where he had a mistress and also had 'dalliances' in England, which were some compensation for what appears to be a loveless marriage.

A possible dalliance of a completely different sort occurred in 1938 when a serial blackmailer, Patrick Tuellman, tried to kidnap Nuffield for a £100,000 ransom. But Tuellman had an accomplice who betrayed his plans to the Oxford City Police. The police briefed Nuffield who was thoroughly intrigued and insisted on attending every meeting. On 28th May the police ambushed Tuellman in Cowley, and in his car the police found him in possession of two automatic pistols, ammunition and items of disguise. He was convicted and served seven years penal servitude.

Britain's most generous benefactor began in a small way, by enabling parents of borstal boys to visit their children to maintain family links and prevent them from becoming too institutionalised. That was in 1926, the year he also established a Chair of Spanish Studies at Oxford, because he felt there were growing business opportunities in Spain and South America and very few places where people could learn Spanish.

However, it was in the medical field that Nuffield directed many of his early benefactions, a throwback to his desire to study medicine. He gave money to hospitals in Birmingham, Coventry and, of course, Oxford.

The first sizeable donation for the Radcliffe Infirmary in Oxford was in 1924 when he presented them with £90,000, allowing them to expand their facilities. This was followed in 1929 by the acquisition of the Radcliffe Observatory site next door, to enable the Infirmary to build the Nuffield Maternity Home, nurses' homes and an operating theatre on the site. As a result of Nuffield's generosity the 1930s saw the Radcliffe Infirmary transform itself into a leading medical research establishment.

The Wingfield Orthopaedic Hospital received over £70,000 in 1931, which enabled it to be largely rebuilt. In 1939 he endowed £1,200,000 to form the National Provincial Hospital Trust; this led to the founding of BUPA and the establishment of the Nuffield Hospitals. He also at this time manufactured over 5,000 iron lungs which he donated to hospitals in the UK for polio victims. He made regular donations to Guy's Hospital, so much so that it erected a statue of him.

One of Nuffield's most important medical donations helped establish Oxford's Postgraduate Medical School in 1936-37. Totalling £2,200,000, it was given on the condition that one of the new medical charities established was for anaesthetics; Nuffield had a bad reaction to anaesthetics when he had his appendix removed some years earlier.

The largest bequest made by Lord Nuffield was to found The Nuffield Foundation. Established in April 1943 with £10,000,000 of Morris Motors shares, the Nuffield Foundation was, for some time, the largest philanthropic trust in the country. Projects funded included funding two scientists who later became Nobel Prize winners: Patrick Blackett (cosmic radiation) and Dorothy Hodgkin (elucidating the structures of penicillin and vitamin B12).

The Lovell Telescope at Jodrell Bank received regular donations throughout the 1950s, making Nuffield a major funder of the Space Age.

In October 2015, *Oxford Today*, the university magazine for Oxford alumni world-wide, paid tribute to Nuffield's generosity to individual university colleges, in some cases rescuing them from possible closure. This was certainly the case with St Peter's College, when, in 1934, Nuffield repaid the college's mortgage after its patron, The Church of England's Martyrs' Memorial Trust, was nearly wiped out by the Great Crash. It could not make its payments on the £70,000 mortgage secured against the college buildings. Lord Nuffield saved the day with a donation of £10,000. In 1936 he made further payments of £62,161. The trigger for his generosity was gratitude for the very moving funeral for his mother, Emily Morris, conducted by the Master of St Peter's, the Revd Christopher Chavasse. As a result the college was rescued from almost certain closure by Nuffield and there arose the Emily Morris Building in her memory, together with a beautiful bronze effigy in the entrance hall.

In 1937, cash-strapped Pembroke and Worcester Colleges each received £50,000, the same year he conceived his own college, the eponymous Nuffield College. Initially he had intended it as a specialist college for engineering, a synergy fitting perfectly with his lifetime achievements as the great industrialist, and much-needed in Oxford. However, what emerged was a postgraduate college for social studies.

His nephew, in an essay about his uncle many years later, called the college "the greatest disappointment of his life, his million pound disappointment, a victim of Oxford's ivory tower attitudes". The puzzle remains that smooth-talking by the academics persuaded the hard-nosed businessman to switch from engineering to social studies. CP Snow's novel *The Master* was clearly a reflection of the Nuffield College experience. Intellectual arrogance, genuine conversion and subsequent disillusionment is probably the simple answer.

However, the fact remains that his achievements in industry and philanthropic causes have touched the lives of hundreds of thousands of people.

— 50 —
Treasure from the Caribbean

The old library of All Souls, dating from the college's foundation in 1438, reflected the college's academic interests: Theology, Law and Medicine. By the early 1700s, however, the old library was filled to capacity and it was indeed fortuitous and timely that Christopher Codrington, in 1710, made a bequest of £10,000 for the building of a new library.

Christopher Codrington (1668-1710) was the son of a wealthy plantation owner and Governor General of the Leeward Islands. He was a graduate of Christ Church and was a Fellow of All Souls from 1690 until 1697. During this time, he turned to the profession of arms and campaigned in the West Indies and Flanders. In 1699 the solider-poet-scholar succeeded to his father's estates and his position as Governor General of the Leeward Islands. After early military and naval success against the French he failed in the Guadeloupe campaign in 1703 and was removed from public office.

Thereafter, Codrington concentrated his energies on theological and philosophical studies and amassed a huge library. After his death in 1710, as well as an endowment of £10,000, All Souls received his library of over 12,000 volumes. Codrington College in Barbados was also created from a bequest made by him.

The architect, Nicolas Hawksmoor, was in the process of putting together designs for the Great Quadrangle at All Souls at the time of Christopher Codrington's death. He rapidly revised his plans to incorporate an extensive new library along the northern boundary of the college site. The 200-foot-long room of the library was completed in 1720 and was the first ground floor academic library in England.

— 51 —

British Prime Minister and Chancellor of Oxford University

1963

The catastrophe which was the First World War (1914-1918) had a seminal and deeply felt effect on not only the university but also on Britain as a whole. Things would never be the same again and the old order of class and privilege was to change forever. Over 14,000 Oxford men went to that bloody conflict of whom 2,700 died. Amongst those who survived was future British Prime Minister, Harold Macmillan (1894-1986).

Macmillan, who entered Balliol in 1912, had his studies interrupted in 1914 when he went to serve King and Country and was wounded three times. The suffering and deprivation he witnessed both in the war and later in the Great Depression of 1930 was to have a profound effect upon him and defined his political credo. Later, in 1957, he was the first Conservative Prime Minister to serve as a one-nation Tory ("You've never had it so good"). He retired somewhat prematurely in 1963 due to ill health. He was Chancellor of Oxford University from 1960 until his death in 1986, and the first serving British Prime Minister to hold this office.

It is an interesting fact that since the Second World War there have been 15 British Prime Ministers, 11 of whom were educated at Oxford University, none from Cambridge University. In chronological order they were:

1945-51	Clement Atlee	(University College)
1955-57	Anthony Eden	(Christ Church)
1957-63	Harold Macmillan	(Balliol College)
1963-64	Alexander Douglas Hume	(Christ Church)
1964-70	Harold Wilson	(Jesus College)
1970-74	Edward Heath	(Balliol College)
1974-76	Harold Wilson	(Jesus College)

1979-90	Margaret Thatcher	(Somerville College)
1997-2007	Tony Blair	(St Johns College)
2010-2016	David Cameron	(Brasenose College)
2016-2019	Theresa May	(St Hughes College)
2019-	Boris Johnson	(Balliol College)

— 52 —

A Yank in Oxford

1931

Arthur Lehman Goodhart KBE, QC, FBA was the first American and the first Jew to be elected Head of an Oxford or Cambridge College when in October 1951 he was elected Master of University College Oxford (Univ).

He was no stranger to Univ having been Professor of Jurisprudence at the University of Oxford 1931-51, when he was also a Fellow of University College.

Arthur Goodhart was born in New York coming from a very wealthy family, his maternal grandfather was Mayer Lehman, one of three brothers who co-founded the world-famous investment banking firm Lehman Brothers. As a result, he was also one of Univ's greatest benefactors, giving the college almost one million dollars over the course of his lifetime (over £6,000,000 in today's terms).

He was educated at Yale University before coming to the UK to continue his education at Trinity College Cambridge. After returning to the United States he practised law until World War I, when he became a member of the US Forces attaining the rank of Captain, when the US joined the war in 1917.

After the war Goodhart returned to England and was called to the Inner Temple in 1919. He became a fellow of Corpus Christi College Cambridge and university lecturer in jurisprudence. In 1931 he moved to Oxford to become Professor of Jurisprudence and a fellow of University College.

It was during the Second World War that he made his greatest contribution to Britain, by lecturing on the radio both here and in the USA. He had connections in the top echelons of the American Government and succeeded in gaining American support for Britain in the early part of the Second World War. He was awarded an honoury KBE (Knighthood) for this singular service.

Both he and his wife, Cecily, were of English ancestry and he was a true Anglophile; his three sons also made significant contributions to public life in Britain. William Goodhart, Lord Goodhart of Youlbury (1933-2017) was an eminent barrister and liberal politician; Sir Philip Goodhart (born 1935) was a Conservative member of Parliament, and Charles Goodhart CBE (born 1936) is an eminent British economist and was a member of the Bank of England Monetary Policy Committee (1997-2000).

Like their father they all attended Trinity College Cambridge. Their father, Arthur Lehman Goodhart, was Master of University College Oxford from 1951-1963 and his lasting legacy to Univ were the buildings he erected, including a new dining hall. The Arlington Room, and the Student Accommodation block, called The Goodhart Building.

After his retirement in 1963, Arthur Goodhart remained in residence at Univ in a Penthouse Suite on top of his Goodhart Building until his death on 10th November 1978. He remained an American Citizen until his death but his lasting legacy were his academic achievements, help to Britain in her hour of need, and above all sons who all made significant contributions to British public life in their particular fields.

— 53 —

Blackwells – a Family Institution

1869

If asked to name the bookshop possessing the largest single room selling books in the world, most people would go for retail book giants like Barnes and Noble in New York, The House of Books in St Petersburg or the Piccadilly branch of Waterstones in London. However, they would be wrong. According to the "Guinness Book of Records" the answer would be the much older Blackwell's Bookshop in Oxford.

Its underground Norrington Room, behind its modest Broad Street façade, occupies a 10,000 square feet space containing 3 miles of shelving. Built in 1966 it extends under the foundations of Trinity College South East Corner and is named after Trinity's President at that time, Sir Arthur Norrington, founder of the eponymous Norrington Table of intercollegiate examination results.

It is all a far cry from the tiny book shop Benjamin Blackwell opened in 1879 at 50 Broad Street. Measuring twelve feet square and able to accommodate just one customer at a time the shop grew in size and stature, occupying adjoining buildings and has since become a national institution.

Sir Basil Blackwell, son of the founder of the business, graduated from Merton College and was chairman of B.H. Blackwell Ltd, known throughout the trade as the gaffer. He was knighted in 1956 and became an honorary fellow of Merton College. He died in 1984 aged 95.

Blackwell's now employs over 1,000 people spread over its chain of 45 shops, which now includes Cambridge, most prestigious bookshop Heffers, which it acquired in 1999.

Although still controlled by the Blackwell family in the guise of Julian "Toby" Blackwell, great-grandson of the founder, Blackwell's is now owned by its employees similar to that of the retailer John Lewis. "Toby" was a graduate of Trinity College, next door to the shop.

In celebration of the 125th anniversary of Blackwell's foundation Julian

"Toby" Blackwell generously donated the firm's archive to Merton College, where Sir Basil – the first in the family to go to university – was an undergraduate in 1906. The Merton Blackwell Collection records tales of generations of Blackwell's found among their dairies and papers, and provides an historical record of the company's development.

There is a north country saying "Clogs to Clogs in four generations" referring to family businesses that have been run by the same family for that length of time, but not Blackwell's. It is a progressive and eclectic mix of the old and the new including Blackwell's online and was one of the first retailers to launch Nook ereader.

Malcolm Horton

— 54 —

Oxbridge
A Public Relations Dream

1849

Oxford and Cambridge are Britain's two oldest universities and are known collectively as "Oxbridge" because it succinctly sums up the fact that they share unique characteristics. Their collegiate systems are much admired all over the world but have never been successfully copied elsewhere.

Oxford has thirty-nine colleges whilst Cambridge has thirty-one with a total student population of 22,000 and 18,000 respectively. All students are members of a college which selects them in the first place, hosts them (accommodates and feeds them) and crucially supervises their studies, often on a one-to-one basis with their college tutor who is an expert in their chosen field of study.

However, it is the University that administers the main lectures and examinations. The reasons they share this unique factor is related to the manner of their respective foundations.

Oxford, founded in 1169, spawned Cambridge in 1209 when a group of Oxford Students, 3000 in number, broke away from Oxford and decamped to Cambridge. The cause of this exodus was the first of the legendary Town versus Gown riots, which took place in Oxford between the resident townspeople and the interlopers, the arrogant new university incomers.

Cambridge was chosen because the leader of the exodus Dr John Grim, an eminent theologian, was born and bred in this relatively insignificant town. It was in terms of structure a copy of Oxford, hence their similarities.

The term Oxbridge highlights this uniqueness shared by the two universities. However the term is, surprisingly, of fairly recent origin first appearing in W.M. Thackery's (Vanity Fair) novel "Pendennis" first published in 1849. Oxbridge was a fictional university in one place whilst the other university was Camford. Quite why Oxbridge caught on and is part of everyday jargon and Camford has not, has something to do with phonetics and is known as a portmanteau word (smog and brunch are other examples). Interestingly the real Oxbridge is a hamlet in Dorset. There does not appear to be a place called Camford although there is a football team in Felin Foel, a small village near Llanelli, called Camford FC which was originally the works team of Fisher & Ludlow. However, Felin Foels most prized asset is its Felin Foel Brewery, home of Double Dragon Ale, the oldest brewery in Wales.

Criticism is often levelled at Oxbridge for its implications of elitism academically and socially as exemplified by figures released in December 2018. They show that whilst only 7% of UK pupils attend private schools, 42% of Oxbridge places go to private schools, particularly Eton College, Westminster School and Magdalen College School.

The parents of these privileged, privately educated children must be delighted that their annual investment in their offspring's education, around £45,000, seems to be paying off. Oxford and Cambridge are making efforts to up the ratio of state school entrants. In 2019-20 Cambridge increased state school freshers from 12% to 14%. But the most discouraging factor must be the cost of keeping a child at Oxbridge, which is about £25,000 a year, which wealthier parents can easily afford. Working class parents not so! So, until we return to free higher education the balance between state school entrants and privately educated children is not likely to change significantly.

On a lighter note, quadrangles, the open spaces surrounded on four sides by buildings such as the college chapel, dining hall and student rooms are called Quads in Oxford, but Courts in Cambridge. And of course, both have topographical landscapes that have been designed by the best architects and landscape gardeners of the day, Christopher Wren, Gilbert Scott and Capability Brown to name but a few. As a result, they are probably, next to London, the UK's greatest tourist attractions, as the crocodiles of tourists filling the narrow lanes bears witness. Oxbridge is indeed unique.

Malcolm Horton

— 55 —

The Downfall of a King and an Oxford Master: James II and Obadiah Walker

1688

The main gate tower of Oxford's oldest College University (Univ) possesses, in a niche facing the main Quadrangle, one of only two statues to be built in England (the other is in Trafalgar Square) of that "foolish" monarch James II. He had succeeded his brother Charles II in 1685 and ruled for only three years; removed by a total rebellion of not only Parliament but the population at large, because they feared a return to popery and divine sovereign rule.

Obadiah Walker, the Master of University College, approved the installation of the Statue in 1687, the year he and the college played host to James II. James converted to Catholicism in 1685 and Obadiah a year later.

Until this time Obadiah Walker had enjoyed a glittering career at Oxford and his alma mater University College, where he had been a scholar, a distinguished Fellow, and finally Master, for over 50 years. He had written many books including what became an unofficial teaching bible "Of education, especially young gentlemen" published in 1673, which ran to five editions. He had travelled widely in Europe and helped found the Ashmolean Museum.

Obadiah's most public act of popery was to turn some rooms in the Master's Lodgings into a Catholic chapel and then as this grew too small, he used a vacant room on the ground floor of the east range of the Quadrangle and made this into a Catholic chapel, which was later expanded. Thus the College had two chapels, the other Anglican. He was also given a royal licence to print and sell thirty-six specified books of Roman Catholic Theology.

In 1688, James II exempted, by Royal Decree, the Masters and Fellows of University College from the provisions of the Religious Tests which, since 1588, had made it illegal to belong to the Roman Catholic Church.

Obadiah's fate was now inextricably linked to that of his monarch.

Unfortunately for Obadiah, James II's aims went beyond Catholicism.

He was making the same mistakes as his father Charles I: supremacy of the Monarchy over Parliament. He was using a return of Catholicism as the thin end of the wedge. He removed all Protestants from positions of power in Oxford, with Obadiah's connivance, he appointed a Catholic as Dean of Christ Church and removed the President and Fellows of Magdalen College and replaced them with his own Catholic appointees. There was no subtlety or political acumen about his actions. Even his own daughters did not support his Catholic ambitions, being staunch Protestants. One, Mary, was married to her cousin the Protestant William Prince of Orange ruler of Holland.

The English ruling classes invited William to England to assume the English throne alongside Mary. He landed in Brixham on 5th November 1688 with his army but encountered no resistance because James' army had deserted.

James was now on the run, followed by his staunch supporter Obadiah Walker. They were on their way to France to seek refuge but were arrested, Obadiah in Sittingbourne and James in Faversham. James escaped and made it to France whilst Obadiah Walker was taken to the Tower of London. There he remained until 2nd June 1690 when, having discharged his bail, was released and spent some time on the continent, and after his return resided in London in poor circumstances. One of his pupils Dr John Radcliffe (of Radcliffe Camera and Observatory fame), a rich physician, supported him. As he grew more infirm he found asylum in Radcliffe's house where he died at the age of 82 and was buried in St Pancras' Churchyard. A sad ending for one of Oxford's finest.

James II spent the rest of his life in France as a guest of Louis XIV and made one serious attempt to win back his throne by launching an attack in Ireland, "The Battle of the Boyne" in July 1690, where he was defeated by his nephew William of Orange.

James returned to France where he died in 1701, and the supremacy of Parliament was never again to be challenged by a ruling monarch.

— 56 —

The Earl of Rochester
The Libertine

1647

John Wilmot, second Earl of Rochester (1647-1680), is one of Wadham College's most distinguished alumni. Today it is rather proud to acknowledge that fact, but it wasn't always so for reasons which will be explained. Suffice to say for the moment, that in 2004 a film was made featuring the controversial Rochester entitled "The Libertine" starring the charismatic American actor Johnny Depp, whose fey and eccentric persona fits the subject of the film and the period in which he lived.

The period in question was the so-called Restoration Period occasioned by the return of Charles II to claim his crown. A time of unrestrained bacchanalia; wine, women and more women, a complete contrast to the previous ten years of the Cromwell/Commonwealth Interregnum of sobriety and piety; Puritanism.

Nowhere was this outpouring more freely expressed than Oxford, which the returning king's father Charles I had made his campaign headquarters during the English Civil War (1642-1649) with Cromwell's Parliamentarians.

The University was firmly Royalist, and as a result suffered great financial deprivation as it sought to accommodate and finance not only a standing army but a King and his court. So, Oxford University being so pro-royalist celebrated the return of the monarchy with extra vigour.

Young John Wilmot, aged only 12, came up to Oxford and Wadham College in January 1660, the same year as Charles II returned from refuge in France. Rochester was in at the beginning of the Restoration transformation when Oxford became a place of huge contrasts, on the one hand debauchery and hedonism, and on the other rich in philosophical and literary achievement. Don't forget Christopher Wren had, a few years earlier, been a student at Wadham College and then a fellow at All Souls, before being appointed

Savilian Professor of Astronomy at Oxford University.

Rochester immersed himself in all aspects of life at Oxford, both intellectual and bacchanalia, laying the foundations for both literary achievement and later his death from syphilis. He became acquainted with a Merton College don, Robert Whitehall, who had a profound effect on young Rochester. Whitehall would lend Rochester his academic gown so that his protégé could visit the taverns and fleshpots and return home undetected by the Proctors (university police). They were undoubtably intimately acquainted and they remained lifelong friends.

Charles II took young Rochester under his wing, and when he left Oxford at the end of 1681 he was immediately sent on a Grand Tour of Europe. This act of almost godfatherly devotion was due to the fact that Rochester's father, Henry Wilmot, engineered Charles II's escape to France at the end of the Civil War, including hiding him in the famous oak tree. It also meant that young Rochester could get away with murder with his outrageous behaviour and insults, such was Charles II's gratitude to Rochester's father who, incidentally, he created 1st Earl of Rochester.

Young Rochester's time in France and Italy exposed him to French and Italian writing and thought, crucial to his development as a poet.

On his return from Europe in 1684, Rochester made his formal debut in Charles II's Restoration Court. It was to Oxford that Charles II decamped to hold his 1665 parliament. The camp followers included Rochester, who had only just completed a period of incarceration in the Tower of London. His crime was that of trying to abduct a young heiress Elizabeth Mallet (both of them underage), who later became his wife.

However, this was the first of many banishments from court due to his continually insulting his Monarch by his actions and satirical verses such as

"We have a pretty witty king
Whose word no man relies on
He never said a foolish thing
Nor ever did a wise one."

Altogether in his lifetime he wrote over 75 poems, of which his most famous was "A Satyr against Reason and Mankind". He also took a great interest in the theatre, particularly young actresses. Nell Gwynn was a mistress long before Charles II set eyes on her and whisked her away. His most well-known work for the theatre was "Sodom, or Quintosole of Debauchery" which however gave rise to prosecution for obscenity. During this time, he took great interest in the career of Elizabeth Barry, a young aspiring actress he coached and who was to become the most famous actress of her time. He took her as a mistress and their affair lasted 5 years.

Sadly, in 1680 aged only 33, he died from syphilis and since his death his work has gone from being classed as the drunken ramblings of a debauched rake, a view shared by Samuel Johnson, to "verses that cut and sparkle like diamonds," the opinion by essayist and critic William Haslitt a century later, whilst Ezra Pound, the 20th century poet and critic, thought he ranked "with Alexander Pope (1688-1744) and John Milton (1608-1674) as one of the greatest poets of his age. He was a man of his time, and like many creative people lived life to the full with antennae fully switched on absorbing all the emotions of life which he expressed in his poems.

— 57 —

The Gay World of Evelyn Waugh

1922

Oxford between the two World Wars was a place of social rebellion and experimentation. The old order was being challenged by the bright young things of the 1920s. Literature, politics and sex were all areas where free expression was practised without any due deference to elders and Evelyn Waugh was at the forefront of this revolution.

At the same time Oxford still retained its traditional appeal as expressed by one of Waugh's fictional characters, Charles Ryder, in his most famous novel "Brideshead Revisited": "Oxford in those days was still a city of aquatint, her autumnal mists, her grey spring time, and the rare glory of her summer days when the chestnut was in flower and the bells ring out high over her gables and cupolas, exhaled the soft vapours of a thousand years of learning."

Waugh had totally fallen in love with Oxford and all that it had to offer, when he spent a week there taking his entrance exams, and was moved to write later "that this last week (in Oxford) has been one of the happiest I have ever known."

He passed his entrance exams with flying colours and entered Hertford College in 1922, the fifth generation of Waugh's to matriculate from Oxford. Despite lack of academic success, due to devoting little time to study, securing a poor third, Oxford was to have a lasting effect on his life and his writing. It gave birth to two quintessential Oxford novels "Decline and Fall" and his magnus opus "Brideshead Revisited".

Waugh was born in 1903 and came from a literary family. His father, Arthur, was a writer and Managing Director and Chairman of the publishing house Chapman and Hall; his elder brother Alec famously wrote "Loom of Youth" and "Island in the Sun", which was made into a film with Harry Belafonte. "Loom of Youth" caused much opprobrium from his alma mater Sherborne School. Published shortly after he left the school and joined the army it "lifted the lid" so to speak on life at a typical public school. Sporting achievement reigned supreme, especially inter-house rivalries, and took precedence over academic achievement. Brutality and homosexuality were prominent features of daily life, with younger boys subjected to much humiliation particularly through the fagging tradition. As a result, Alec's younger brother Evelyn was virtually barred from attending Sherbourne, and Lancing College was chosen because it was high church Anglican firmly based on sound principles in the Christian faith. It was the first of the Woodard Schools founded by the Rev'd Nathaniel Woodard in 1848. He went on to found 29 more. It was seen by Evelyn's father as an antidote to Sherbourne, but probably denied him entry into the more prestigious colleges at Oxford.

There then ensued a life of total debauchery and hedonism. His life seen through an alcoholic haze involved a succession of homosexual affairs and "getting in" with the wrong sort: rich spoilt brats from Eton and other leading public schools, being a total snob this suited Evelyn. He joined the notorious Bullingdon Club where excessive drinking and near riotous and secretary behaviours were the order of the day. He was also a member of the Hypocrites Club, a harem for homosexuals. His friends included Harold Acton, the outrageously gay poet who was the inspiration for Anthony Blanche in "Brideshead". Tom Driberg, later to become a controversial Labour MP and insatiable homosexual, was another close friend.

Waugh's history tutor CRMF Cruttwell was infuriated by Waugh's behaviour and lack of academic application, leading to the two men's mutual loathing culminating in the infamous accusation that Cruttwell was a dog sodomist!

Evelyn only attained a third-class degree, but Oxford, as has been, said had a profound effect on his future writing career. He left Oxford in 1925 and embarked on a series of teaching jobs befitting for a man with only a third-class degree.

In 1928, Evelyn having outgrown his homosexual phase, common to many public schoolboys, married the eponymous Evelyn Gardner daughter of Lord and Lady Burghdere who fiercely opposed the marriage to no avail. His wife left him in 1928 which coincided with publication of his first novel "Decline and Fall."

Waugh then embarked on his series of series of satirical novels: "Vile Bodies" (1930), "A Handful of Dust (1934), "Black Mischief" (1934), Scoop (1938), as well as getting married again in 1936 to Laura Herbert a union which produced seven children and lasted nearly 30 years until his death.

The outbreak of the Second World War saw him at the age of 36 enlist in the Royal Marines and then the SAS. His peregrinations took him to Sierra Leone, and then a dull period in Gibraltar as mail censor where he wrote the cynical "Put out more Flags" (1942). Next, he moved on to Crete which the British tamely surrendered to the Germans, much to Waugh's disgust. However, it was to provide much valuable source material for his "Sword of Honour Trilogy," begun in 1952 with "Men at Arms" It was later made into a television film with Daniel Craig (2001).

It was during a period of convalescence from a parachuting accident from December 1944 to June 1945 that he wrote his magus opus "Brideshead Revisited." The hero Chares Ryder has much in common with its author; like many of his books they are semi-autobiographical as is his penultimate book "The Ordeal of Gilbert Pinfold" (1957), about a writer going mad under the influence of drugs and alcohol.

His last major work was "Unconditional Surrender," (1961) the final part of the Sword of Honour Trilogy. He was old beyond his years due to a lifetime of heavy drinking and drugs and died of heart failure at the age of 62.

There is no doubt that together with Anthony Powell he was one of the greatest writers of the 20th century; both were Oxonians and drew their inspiration as writers from the "City of Dreaming Spires".

ID # 58 —

The Killer Queen of Spies

1961

Although she didn't have a licence to kill Baroness Park, CMG, OBE, FRS Principal of Somerville College (1980-1989) admitted, just before she died in 2010, that when based in Leopoldville as an M16 operative she arranged in 1961, the kidnap and execution of Patrice Lumumba the Congo's first democratically elected prime minister.

Daphne Park born in South Africa in 1922 spent her childhood living in a tin roof shack in Dares Salaam, Tanzania and after an extraordinary career as an M16 operative from 1943 to 1979, she became Baroness Park.

Her career in the Secret Intelligence Services (SIS) MI6 spanned the Second World War and the Cold War that followed, culminating in her becoming in 1970, Controller of the Western Hemisphere, the highest post achieved, at that time, by a woman in the Secret Intelligence Services.

On graduating from Somerville College Oxford in 1943 she became a coding expert in the Special Operational Executive (SOE).

After the war she joined M16 with stints in Vienna, Moscow (she was a fluent Russian speaker) Leopoldville (The Congo) Lusaka (Zambia) Hanoi (then North Vietnam) and Outer Mongolia.

Hers was an extraordinary life serving in hostile environments where she was tortured, faced down a machete welding mob and forced to live in a rat-infested shack in North Vietnam. She smuggled out British Nationals from troubled hot spots particularly the Congo for which she received the OBE. But the assassination of Patricia Lumumba, in the wake of the Belgium abandonment of the Congo, is the most crucial operation Daphne Parker carried out to secure the Congo's rich uranium deposits for The West. They were used in the Americas atomic bombs in World War Two. Patrice Lumumba's communist leanings would have almost certainly led to the uranium ending up in the hands of the Russians, so he had to be removed!

Daphne Park's natural charm and unflappability allied to her appearance a small well rounded Miss Marple type figure saw her through the most challenging situations in the Cold War environment in which she operated.

— 59 —

"Women Have a Lesser Brain" Charles Darwin

1920

Women were not awarded degrees at Oxford until 1920, when Emily Penrose, Principal of Somerville College, became the first woman to be presented with a BA; 700 years after the foundation of the university!

In fact, women were not allowed to study at Oxford until 1878 when the first female college, Lady Margaret Hall, was founded by Elizabeth Wordsworth, great-niece of the poet William Wordsworth. Further ladies' colleges quickly followed: Somerville in 1879, St Hughes in 1886 and St Hilda's in 1843.

Why had it taken so long for women to be admitted to Oxford? The attitude to women can best be summed up by no lesser expert on the development of the human race than Charles Darwin's who in 1859 opined "that the woman's brain was less highly developed than that of a man's, a characteristic of the lower races". A disciple of Darwin, Herbert Spencer went even further and expressed the view that "all brain forcing of woman produced neurosis, chlorosis, hysteria, dwarfism and flat chests and as a result they could never bear a well-developed infant". Such remarks today would cause a riot.

Initially, women could not become full members of the university even though they sat the same exams. They were given diplomas instead of degrees. In 1914 Lord Curzon, Chancellor of Oxford University and former Viceroy of India, despatched his famous Scarlett letter to the University recommending that its women be admitted to the degree of BA.

But the deciding factor was the First World War which was the catalyst for the seismic change to the social fabric of this country, including women's place in society. In Oxford's case the absence of tutors called up for active service meant that women tutors stood in for absent male tutors and acquitted themselves most ably. In 1920, once the war, was over a grateful Congregation (University ruling body) readily agreed to award women degrees.

Unknown Oxford

However, women were confined to the four female colleges until 1974 when five all-male colleges Brasenose, Hertford, Jesus, Wadham and St Catherine's admitted women. Interestingly, it was the women's colleges that were reluctant to let men cross their threshold. However, starting with St Hughes in 1986 they began admitting men, with finally St Hilda's succumbing in 2008.

In contrast Cambridge did not award women degrees until 1948 even though it was Cambridge that founded the first female college, Girton, in 1869, nearly ten years before Oxford. Also, the last female-only college will not be allowing males across its threshold until 2021.

At the moment six of the thirty-nine heads of college are women and Oxford has produced four female prime ministers: Indira Gandhi, Margaret Thatcher, Benazir Bhutto and Theresa May.

The full emancipation of Oxford is now complete with the number of students of either sex being about equal. Darwin must be turning in his grave but then again, he was a product of the "other place," Cambridge.

60

Adam Von Trott The Rhodes Scholar who tried to Assassinate Hitler

1944

Adam Von Trott was a German Rhodes Scholar at Balliol College from 1931 to 1933. He was executed on 26th August 1944 for his leading part in the plot to assassinate Adolph Hitler in July 1944.

He had previously attended Oxford University during the Hilary Term of 1929 studying Theology at Mansfield College and became a great friend of the historian A.L. Rowse. He developed a great love for Oxford and its intellectual freedom. As a result, he returned in 1931 as a Rhodes Scholar.

Von Trott was a man possessing great charisma and charm being part of the Hessian dynasty that had ruled Hesse for over 600 years. He was distantly related to the Duke of Edinburgh.

Being an idealist, he detested the Nazi Philosophy with pedigree and charm he quickly made friends with Oxfords great and the good including the philosopher Issiah Berlin, Maurice Bowra, David Astor, Sandie Lindsay the Master of Balliol and Shelia Grant Duff. His old friend A.L. Rowse who was gay developed an intense infatuation for the heterosexual Von Trott calling him one of the most beautiful intelligent and charming men he had ever met. However, such feelings were not reciprocated. In any case Von Trott was deeply in love with Sheila Grant Duff and even proposed to her with no success; she was already engaged.

Much to the disappointment of his friends he returned to Germany and worked his way up in Hitler's regime playing the part of a double agent, because he was a member of the Kreisau Circle opposed to Hitler and Nazism. He even visited Britain as Hitler's envoy in 1939 to sound out Prime Minister Neville Chamberlain and Foreign Secretary Lord Halifax on the Polish Situation. Whilst also making unofficial contacts on behalf of the resistance group. However, he was greatly misunderstood by his Oxford Friends who assumed he had become a fully paid up Nazi.

Unknown Oxford

A great friend of Von Trott's was Christabel Bielenberg, an English woman and niece of Lord Northcliffe, who was married to Peter Bielenberg a German lawyer, they were also members of the Kreisau circle.

A letter Von Trott wrote to her in 1944 just before his death, sums up the ambivalence. Von Trott's Oxford friends felt towards him which he couldn't understand.

"I owe more to Oxford than I can say, but it's a strange thing, when I decided to come back to Germany in 1933, I would have thought I did exactly what most of my Oxford friends would have done if they were faced with Hitler in their own country. Yet the very fact that I did come back aroused, I think nothing but distrust – damaging distrust. I sometimes wonder how many friends I have there now – I mean real friends".

However, it was an earlier letter written to the Manchester Guardian in 1934 that convinced his Oxford friends that he really was a Nazi. In the letter he said that in his experience Jews were not discriminated against in the legal process. In fact, he wrote, he had talked to some brown shirts, who asserted that they would never mistreat Jews. Von Trott's letter was absolutely wrong and it was the turning point for Issiah Berlin and most of his Oxford friends.

However, David Astor suggested that Von Trott was establishing his cover as a double agent.

The damage was done, and, on his death, Maurice Bowra wrote "That's one Nazi who was hanged". However, when some years later the true nature of his anti-Nazi activities emerged both Berlin and Bowra openly confessed to having misjudged Von Trott.

Initially both Balliol and Rhodes House ignored his death but made amends some years later. Von Trott is one of the five Germans who are common orated on the World War II memorial stone at Baliol College. In the Rotunda of Rhodes his name is also recorded among the Rhodes Scholars war dead.

— 61 —

Other Oxfords

2019

In an episode of the television series "Morse" entitled " " the university Chancellor played by John Gielgud asserts that there are many Oxfords worldwide. In fact, there are eighteen with no less than fourteen in the United States. There is only one other Cambridge Worldwide in Massachusetts. It's the home to Harvard University.

Collectively they are often referred to as "Oxbridge", but this is a comparatively recent phenomenon, first appearing in Thackeray's novel Pendennis in 1849. Oxbridge was a fictional university in one place whilst the other was Camford. Quite why Oxbridge has caught on and is part of everyday jargon and Camford has not, has something to do with phonetics and it is now known as a portmanteau word ('smog' and 'brunch' are other examples) which is a morphological blend. Interestingly, the real Oxbridge is a hamlet in Dorset. There does not appear to be a place called Camford.

An article under the heading Exporting Oxford appeared in the 1998 Hilary edition of the University magazine Oxford Today. It discussed attempts to replicate the unique elements of Oxford's collegiate system and architecture overseas.

One of the places mentioned was the University of the South, Sewanee, which is situated 2,500 feet above sea level on a plateau in central Tennessee. Its campus is an oasis of tranquillity set in 10,000 acres of the most beautiful woodland, with breath taking views all around.

Founded by the leaders of the Episcopal Church in 1857, it has a student population limited to 1,400 with a teaching ratio of only 9:1. It has always had close links with the Church of England and Oxford University.

The integrity of gothic architecture is amazing. One of its earliest structures, the Breslin Tower (1886), was modelled on Magdalen Tower, Oxford, and all subsequent buildings have remained faithful to the gothic style, including the $12,000,000 Dining Hall which was recently completed.

Unknown Oxford

The painting featured here is of the Sharpard Tower which in 1959 completed the cathedral-like All Saints Chapel started in 1907. The tower was modelled on St Mary the Virgin, Oxford although the spire was changed to a lantern. Most of the chapel's stained glass including a magnificent 20-foot diameter rose window, was executed by J Wippel and Co Limited of Exeter, in England, in 1958. The building to the right of the chapel is the eastern side of th4e Carnegie Hall, completed in 1913.

The University of the South maintains close links with Oxford, having summer schools each year in both Lincoln College and St John's College.

Malcolm Horton

— 62 —

A Stroll around the Universities' Colleges

2019

Finally, to put these tales into perspective, a comfortable circular walk of just under three miles can encompass 20 of Oxford University's principal colleges. The starting point is Magdalen Bridge, which has, appropriately, been the place where notable visitors were welcomed or took their official departure from the city, as did Queen Elizabeth I in 1556.

Entering Oxford across the bridge, one immediately sees the bell tower of Magdalen College. It becomes the centre of worldwide attention on May Day morning, when the thronging masses below listen to the choir on high sing a welcome to the coming summer.

Magdalen, founded in 1458, boasts many distinguished literary and musical alumni. Oscar Wilde gained a double first, whereas Poet Laureate John Betjeman was rusticated (sent down). Ivor Novello sang in the choir and Dudley Moore was an organ scholar.

Once over the bridge, one enters Oxford's famous High Street – 'The High'. On the right is the impressive entrance screen and cupola of Queen's College. It was built by William Townesend in 1734. Queen's is so-called because it was founded in 1341 under the patronage of Edward III's wife, Philippa.

Opposite Queen's is Oxford's oldest college, University College, founded in 1249 and affectionately known as 'Univ'. Its two battlemented gate towers contain statues of the last three Stuart monarchs – Queen Mary II, Queen Anne and King James II. Beyond the gate towers is the dome of the Shelley Memorial under which resides a marble statue of the poet, Percy Bysshe Shelley, who was an undergraduate in 1811. More recent students include the former American President, Bill Clinton.

Crossing back over The High we come to All Souls which is unique in Oxford, having neither graduate nor undergraduate pupils, only Fellows and post-graduate research workers. It was founded in 1438 by Archbishop Chichele to commemorate the dead of the Hundred Years' War with France. All Souls is best viewed by turning right into Catte Street, which also contains architectural gems such as the university church – St Mary the Virgin, and on the opposite corner, James Gibbs' Radcliffe Camera. When constructed in 1748 this was the first round library in Britain.

Opposite All Souls and across the cobbled Radcliffe Square is Brasenose College. It was founded in 1509 on the site of the mediaeval Brasenose Hall from which the college acquired not only its name, but eventually the famous bronze sanctuary knocker or 'brazen nose'.

Across Radcliffe Square is Hertford College, featuring the famous Bridge of Sighs designed by Sir Thomas Jackson and completed in 1914. Originally founded as Hart Hall in 1283, the college closed in 1818 due to lack of funds. In 1874, however, a noted banker, TC Baring, provided an endowment which enabled it to be re-founded.

Passing under the Bridge of Sighs, New College Lane leads to the original entrance of New College, founded in 1379 by William of Wykeham. The Great Quadrangle contains a chapel, hall and library. The other major quadrangle at New College is the Hollywell Quadrangle, completed in 1896 and which incorporates, on its fourth side, the 12th century city wall. This is now the college's main entrance from Holywell Street.

At the end of Holywell Street and to the right is Parks Road along which is Wadham College. It was endowed in 1609 by a wealthy Devonian, Nicholas Wadham, on his death bed. It was, however, his widow, Dorothy, who carried out his wishes. She directed operations from her home in the West Country, but never visited Oxford and so did not see her foundation before she died at the age of 84. The east range of the Front Quadrangle features, above the entrance to the hall, statues of Nicholas and Dorothy Wadham and James I. Inside the hall is a portrait of Sir Christopher Wren who graduated from Wadham in 1653 and whose most famous creation in Oxford is the Sheldonian Theatre.

A further 400 yards along Parks Road, on the left, is Keble College, designed by William Butterfield and founded in 1868. The building has always caused controversy because of its idiosyncratic use of bricks of different colours, making it unlike any other Oxford college. Inside its chapel hangs William Holman Hunt's famous painting *The Light of the World*.

Opposite the back of Keble, in Woodstock Road, is Somerville College which, in 1879, was the second ladies' college to be founded in Oxford.

(Lady Margaret Hall was the first, founded a year earlier.) Somerville was immortalised by a distinguished alumnus, Dorothy L Sayers, in her novel *Gaudy Night*, published in 1935. Another famous scholar was former Prime Minister, Lady Margaret Thatcher. Somerville became a mixed college in 1994, followed in 2008 by Oxford's last remaining female-only college, St Hilda's, which is now also mixed.

Returning towards the centre of Oxford down St Giles Street, on the left-hand side is a college that will forever be associated with the religious turmoil surrounding the reign of Mary I. St John's College was founded in 1555 by a wealthy Roman Catholic clothier, Sir Thomas White, in gratitude for the restoration of Catholicism under Mary I. This led to three prominent Protestants, Bishops Ridley, Latimer and Archbishop Cranmer, being burnt at the stake in Oxford in 1555 and 1556. Their Martyrs' Memorial stands adjacent to the college.

When, however, Mary was succeeded by her Protestant step-sister, Elizabeth, the tide turned and one of St John's first Fellows, Edmund Campion, became Oxford's most celebrated Catholic martyr when, in 1581, he was executed at Tyburn. From then on, Roman Catholics were not officially allowed to attend the university until 1895! It is interesting to note that, in 1980, Tony Blair, a graduate of St John's, married his Roman Catholic bride in the college chapel.

Passing the Martyrs' Memorial and turning left into Broad Street one encounters the Victorian eminence of Balliol. Although founded in 1263 it was virtually rebuilt from the middle of the 19th century by a succession of eminent architects – Waterhouse, Butterfield, Keene and Salvin.

Next door to Balliol is Trinity, whose open and spacious Front Quadrangle can be viewed through the railings which front Broad Street. Immediately catching the eye is the 17th century chapel which was the first non-Gothic chapel to be built in Oxford, when it replaced the earlier one dating from the 13th century.

Across Broad Street is one of Oxford's most famous thoroughfares, Turl Street, at the end of which stands the beautiful All Saints' Church. It was declared redundant by the Church Commissioners in 1971 and tastefully converted into Lincoln College Library in 1975.

Three colleges front Turl Street, the first being Exeter College on the left, founded in 1314. In the Front Quadrangle stands the chapel, completed in 1859 and designed by George Gilbert Scott. Inside is a wonderful tapestry designed by Edward Burne-Jones and executed by William Morris, who were both contemporaries of Exeter in the 1850s and leading members of the pre-Raphaelite movement.

Opposite Exeter is Jesus College, which is the only Oxford college to date from the Elizabethan period. In the hall there is a full-length portrait of Queen Elizabeth I by Nicholas Hilliard (1537-1619).

Further down Turl Street, past Brasenose Lane, we come across Lincoln College, on the left, which actually straddles both sides of the street because it owns all of the shops on the right and the 15th century Mitre Hotel. The rooms above the shops have been converted into student accommodation.

Lincoln's most influential scholar was John Wesley, who made the college the cradle of Methodism. From 1726 until 1735 he occupied rooms in Chapel Quad.

At the end of Turl Street, turning right into the High Street, one comes to a crossroads. This is Carfax, the mediaeval centre of Oxford, with its landmark St Michael's Tower.

Turning left down St Aldate's one can see Tom Tower – Christopher Wren's crowning glory of Christ Church. Cardinal College, as it was originally known, was founded by Cardinal Thomas Wolsey in 1525. He was Henry VIII's Chancellor and asset-stripped 22 monasteries to provide funds for his new college, which was to be the grandest in Oxford. Wolsey, however, incurred Henry VIII's displeasure for his extravagant use of power and he was sacked in 1529. Henry then took over and completed the college, renaming it Christ Church in 1546. In the same year, Henry made his Christ Church Cathedral the college chapel. Over a century later, Christopher Wren paid tribute to Thomas Wolsey by naming his ogee-capped bell-tower, Tom Tower.

Passing across the Great Quad of Christ Church and then its Peckwater Quad, one exits the college into Oriel Square.

Opposite is the entrance to Oriel College, founded in 1326 by King Edward II. The present Front Quadrangle, with its hall and chapel, was completely rebuilt and was one of the largest projects in pre-Restoration Oxford. Inexplicably, the architect is unknown.

Charles I used Oxford as his campaign headquarters during the Civil War until his surrender in 1646. Above the entrance portico to the hall can be seen the words 'Regnante Carolo' referring to the fact that Charles I used Oriel for meetings of the Privy Council.

On the corner of Oriel Square and Merton Street is Corpus Christi College, famous for its pelican sundial. Erected in 1581, it celebrates Nicholas Kratzer, a Bavarian who was elected a Fellow of the college in 1517. He introduced horology – the science of measuring time – to England.

Next to Corpus Christi is Merton, founded in 1264 and the first college to have a resident student population. Merton's Mob Quad is the oldest quadrangle in Oxford and contains the oldest working library in the world, dating from 1371. Merton also has an immense chapel, cathedral-like in size with one of the most impressive towers in Oxford.

Turning right along Merton Street, then left down Logic Lane, takes one back to the High Street – opposite Queen's College. A right turn down 'The High' leads back to Magdalen Bridge and the completion of the walk.